Praise for *The Shift That Changes Everything*

This book is an authoritative work written from the heart of firsthand experience. Ted Pagel, in this landmark work, offers a clear road map for overcoming the hurts, hurdles, and hang-ups of life. It's not a guide to survival—it's a guide to winning!

—Dr. Phillip Brassfield
President, Destiny Leaders
Heber Springs, Arkansas

While Allen Saunders taught us that "life is what happens to you while you're busy making other plans," Ted Pagel teaches us how to handle what life throws our way. Ted is no stranger to challenges or the exhilaration of overcoming them. His heart for people and the desire to see them reach their full level of joy jump off the pages of his writings.

—Tommy Brandon
Senior Pastor, Calvary Church
Fort Worth, Texas

Many people think that those people who radiate warmth and light into our lives are either faking it or couldn't possibly have experienced the difficulties and darkness we have faced. While this may be true for the majority of "fake it until you make it" devotees to the power of positive thinking, there are those authentic, rare few whose internal fire and passion are genuine and powerful, not originating in vain theories of men but from a spiritual reality that has sustained them through life's toughest challenges. In this book Ted Pagel draws back the curtain in very personal episodes of intense pain and difficult challenges in his own life, highlighting the effectiveness of building up one's life and character through belief in Christ and following the leading of the Holy Spirit.

He demonstrates that choosing one's attitude is not the result of life's circumstances or confidence in some vain theory of man, but it is a choice of will as a form of worship to God the Father and the Lord Jesus Christ. This choice releases God's working in all things to emerge in life-changing ways in every area of our lives. Yes, there is some truth in the power of positive thinking and attitudes, but it is only a faint shadow of the power that occurs when faith and conviction in the goodness of what God has provided for believers in spiritual realms rise in a person who experiences the leading of Christ through the hardest and darkest challenges of life. The harder the challenges life brings, the more faith grows when we are determined never to be separated from the love of God and life in Christ. The result is that choosing one's attitude is not some enormous exertion of will but the agreeable acknowledgement of the goodness of God in all things, no matter how bittersweet the situation may be. Ted testifies to the true transformative power that attitude brings to shaping one's life, not from theory but from faith, worship, and a genuine relationship with God.

—Dr. Jon Hitchcock
Author
Ocean Springs, Mississippi

In *The Shift That Changes Everything*, Pastor Ted Pagel delivers a powerful and deeply personal guide to navigating life's hardest seasons with grace, resilience, and perspective. This is not just a book—it's a companion for the broken, a guide for the weary, and a charge to those ready to live with purpose in spite of pain. This is a must-read for anyone navigating disappointment, loss, or emotional struggle. Pastors, leaders, and counselors will find it especially valuable. Pastor Pagel writes with empathy, grit, and deep spiritual insight—offering a message that lingers long after the final page.

—Shane Warren
Senior Pastor, The Bend Church
Cookeville, Tennessee

THE SHIFT THAT CHANGES EVERY THING

MANAGING YOUR
ATTITUDE WHEN
LIFE DOESN'T
GO YOUR WAY

THE SHIFT THAT CHANGES EVERY THING

MANAGING YOUR ATTITUDE WHEN LIFE DOESN'T GO YOUR WAY

TED PAGEL JR.
FOREWORD BY CHONDA PIERCE

Harp & Sword
MEDIA

The Shift That Changes Everything by Ted Pagel Jr.
Copyright © 2026 by Ted Pagel Jr.

Published by Harp & Sword Media LLC
129 S. Main St., #260
Grapevine, TX 76051

All rights reserved. No part of this publication may be reproduced, stored in a retrieval system, or transmitted in any form or by any means—electronic, mechanical, photocopy, recording, or otherwise—except for brief quotations in printed reviews, without the prior written permission of the publisher.

Unless otherwise noted, Scripture quotations are taken from the New King James Version®. Copyright © 1982 by Thomas Nelson. Used by permission. All rights reserved.

Scripture quotations marked NIV are taken from the Holy Bible, New International Version®, NIV®. Copyright © 1973, 1978, 1984, 2011 by Biblica, Inc.® Used by permission of Zondervan. All rights reserved worldwide. www.zondervan.com. The "NIV" and "New International Version" are trademarks registered in the United States Patent and Trademark Office by Biblica, Inc.®

Scripture quotations marked ESV are from The ESV® Bible (The Holy Bible, English Standard Version®), © 2001 by Crossway, a publishing ministry of Good News Publishers. ESV® Text Edition: 2016. The ESV text may not be quoted in any publication made available to the public by a Creative Commons license. The ESV may not be translated in whole or in part into any other language. Used by permission. All rights reserved

Scripture quotations marked with the designation "GW" are taken from *GOD'S WORD*®. © 1995, 2003, 2013, 2014, 2019, 2020 by God's Word to the Nations Mission Society. Used by permission.

Cover design by Joe DeLeon of DeLeon Design
Interior formatting by Will Rainier

ISBN: 979-8-9915080-9-4
Ebook ISBN: 979-8-9988032-0-8

10 9 8 7 6 5 4 3 2 1

Printed in the United States of America

This book is dedicated to my mother, Mary Ann Pagel, who taught me so much about life and attitude.

She showed me that life isn't about avoiding the storms but about learning to walk through them with courage, compassion, and conviction. Even in the darkest moments, she found reasons to smile, believe, and love well.

Though she's graduated to heaven, her legacy lives on in me and now in this book.

Mom, thank you for being the example I needed, the strength I leaned on, and the voice I still hear when life gets hard.

CONTENTS

Foreword by Chonda Pierce xi
Introduction xiii

CHAPTER 1	Unexpected Results 1
CHAPTER 2	When Life Is Unfair 19
CHAPTER 3	The Illusion of Control 37
CHAPTER 4	Dealing with Difficult People 55
CHAPTER 5	The Death of a Dream 75
CHAPTER 6	The Power of Words 93
CHAPTER 7	Haunted by the Past 107
CHAPTER 8	Let Setbacks Become Comebacks 125
CHAPTER 9	A New Pair of Glasses 139
CHAPTER 10	The Lifelong Journey 153

Using The Shift That Changes Everything
  in Classes and Groups 165
Acknowledgments 169
Endnotes 171
About the Author 175

FOREWORD

I've been a stand-up comedian for more than thirty-five years—a career built on making others laugh, even when life's difficulties seem overwhelming. Throughout this journey I've had the privilege of knowing Ted Pagel for over forty-five years. Ted's life, ministry, and friendship have profoundly impacted my perspective, continually reminding me that humor and hope often intertwine in the most unexpected ways.

There's a remarkable power that emerges when we share our stories openly and authentically. Our stories aren't merely personal histories; they are vivid testimonies of God's transformative work in our lives. Ted exemplifies this truth. With kindness, vulnerability, and a generous heart, he courageously shares his life's journey, never shying away from revealing his struggles, setbacks, and profound moments of healing.

Ted has endured trials and heartaches that would challenge even the strongest among us. But instead of allowing these experiences to leave him bitter or defeated, he allowed God to reshape and redirect his pain into a purposeful mission. Through this book Ted teaches us essential lessons about attitude and resilience—how guarding our hearts from bitterness and cynicism enables us to fully embrace the future God has designed for us.

Ted not only shares his journey but also provides practical insights and spiritual guidance for overcoming our past hurts. Through his own story Ted illuminates pathways to healing, productivity, and spiritual fulfillment, demonstrating how every experience, no matter how painful, can be woven by God into a beautiful purpose.

This book isn't just Ted's story; it's a blueprint for all of us, a guide to transforming our deepest wounds into significant victories. Whether you're grappling with recent heartbreak or old, persistent scars, Ted's wisdom—drawn from decades of pastoral care and personal experiences—offers fresh hope and practical tools to help you move forward with confidence and purpose.

I'm immensely proud to call Pastor Ted Pagel my friend and deeply excited about the insights and breakthroughs that await each reader in this book. Ted's journey is a testament to God's unwavering faithfulness and the remarkable things He can accomplish when we learn to manage our attitudes, regardless of what life throws at us.

—Chonda Pierce
Christian Comedian
Ashland City, Tennessee

INTRODUCTION

Have you ever noticed how quickly life can shift, without warning, without permission? Perhaps you've experienced moments when the carefully crafted path you envisioned for your life suddenly crumbled, leaving you to navigate uncharted terrain filled with disappointment, frustration, and uncertainty. We've all faced circumstances that didn't align with our expectations, moments when life simply didn't go our way.

What if the greatest tool we have in these challenging moments isn't changing our *circumstances* but changing our *perspective*? What if the key to thriving through difficulty and disappointment is not what happens *around* us but what happens *within* us? This transformative internal adjustment is what I call *the shift that changes everything*.

Throughout my decades of pastoral ministry and personal experience, I've seen firsthand how attitude can make or break our ability to grow, thrive, and find joy, even in the toughest of seasons. Managing your attitude when life doesn't cooperate is more than positive thinking or mere optimism—it's a powerful, biblically grounded decision to trust God's sovereignty, even when the circumstances seem bleak.

This book is designed to guide you through both the spiritual and practical steps to make this crucial internal shift. In each chapter we'll address common struggles—unfairness, difficult relationships, shattered dreams, and past hurts—and discover timeless truths from God's Word that empower you to respond with grace, resilience, and hope.

My prayer is that as you journey through these pages, you'll embrace the freedom that comes when you realize your attitude isn't a hostage to your situation. Instead, it can become your greatest ally, reshaping setbacks into comebacks, struggles into strengths, and pain into purpose.

Welcome to the journey of learning how to manage your attitude—the shift that truly changes everything.

Chapter 1

UNEXPECTED RESULTS

*Eye has not seen, nor ear heard,
nor have entered into the heart of man
the things which God has prepared
for those who love Him.*
—1 Corinthians 2:9

"If you don't leave my mother alone, I'll kill you!"

I'd reached my breaking point. I was thirteen years old, standing in the kitchen, watching my father yell at my mother, calling her names and threatening her. It wasn't the first time. It had happened more times than I could count. But something in me snapped that afternoon. Mom stood nearby, gripping a skillet, clearly ready to defend herself if things escalated. Thankfully, Dad backed off, at least for that moment.

While I was growing up, my father was a complicated man. He was what some would call a "functioning alcoholic." He kept his job, showed up to work, and maintained a respectable image in public. To those outside our home he came across as kind, generous, and even thoughtful. And at times he really

THE SHIFT THAT CHANGES EVERYTHING

was. But behind closed doors, it was a different story. Inside our home, we lived with a man who often let his inner pain and unresolved anger spill out, especially onto my mom.

He frequently accused her of being unfaithful, throwing out cruel and baseless accusations, often naming people in our community and claiming she was involved with them. It was painful and bewildering, especially since we later learned he was the one who had been unfaithful. Looking back, I can see now what I didn't fully understand then: He was deflecting his guilt, projecting his shame. In many ways what we experienced as a family was emotional gaslighting—before I even knew what that word meant.

Life at home could feel like walking on eggshells. My dad worked hard to provide for us, and I'll never take that away from him. But we never knew which version of him would walk through the door each evening. There was a constant tension in the air, as if we were always bracing for the next explosion. He could find fault with just about anything, and no one was immune.

Through all of it Mom remained steady. She didn't grow bitter. Somehow she never let the verbal assaults steal her tenderness. She was everything he wasn't in those moments—calm, resilient, full of grace. She chose love even when it would've been easier to shut down. She was at every one of my games, my biggest cheerleader, and my constant encourager. Her strength was quiet, but it was fierce. She was the safe place in a house that didn't always feel safe.

Eventually, the emotional toll became too much. When I was fifteen, Mom overdosed. We had to call an ambulance and rush her to the hospital. I remember sitting by her side afterward and saying, "Mom, it's not worth it. You need to be somewhere safe." Even after that moment she still chose to stay. She couldn't bring herself to leave our home or our family. And honestly, that only deepened the anger I felt toward my dad. She was the closest thing to an angel I had ever known. She wasn't perfect, but she loved with a kind of courage that still shapes who I am today.

Mom never just rolled over in the face of my father's attacks. She didn't lash out, but she didn't back down either. I remember one time, in the middle of a heated moment, she looked him straight in the eye and said, "You're of the devil." That didn't stop him, but for us kids watching, it showed us she wasn't afraid to tell the truth.

I used to tell myself, "I'll never be like him." I swore I'd take a different path, make different choices, and become a different kind of man. But when I turned sixteen, I remember looking in the mirror one day, and there he was. Not his face, but his posture. His tone. The set of his jaw. I saw traits I had inherited—some good and some hard to face. It was sobering. As much as I had resisted, I couldn't deny that he was a part of me.

That realization shook me. It felt like a crossroads.

Then, not long after, my football coach invited me to a Fellowship of Christian Athletes meeting. Later he brought me to a revival service at Hilldale Baptist Church in Clarksville, Tennessee. That night, the message of grace came alive for me. For the first time I truly understood what Jesus had done—not just for the world but for *me*. I walked to the front and gave my life to Christ, and everything changed.

This wasn't just about heaven or hell. It was about becoming a different man, one who would carry forward the compassion of my mother and the redemptive grace of my Savior. That night marked a new beginning. A fresh start. A decision to break the cycle and become someone who would bring healing, not harm.

COPING STRATEGIES AND GRACE

I've met countless people who suffered abusive family relationships and use various strategies to survive. For some, anger drives them to dominate others. They have to win at all costs to avoid feeling weak and vulnerable. Others become passive, accepting the status of a victim because it feels safer than standing up for themselves. Some are driven to please people. They look for problems they can solve (and there are plenty in their crazy-making families!) so they can feel good about themselves. Still others decide to party their way through life, grabbing as much pleasure as possible, no matter the cost. As we attempt to cope with our traumatic pasts, it becomes easier to avoid honesty or vulnerability and turn to substances or behaviors to numb the pain and distract us from the chaos. It may be as overtly destructive as an opioid addiction or as seemingly benign as watching too much television. By employing these strategies, we intuitively strive to achieve two goals: self-protection and finding some sort of meaning; however, these unhealthy coping mechanisms inevitably lead to more manipulation, fear, demands, and heartache.

Most of us go to great lengths to avoid being vulnerable. We wear masks to hide our insecurity, and we try to impress people enough so they don't ask probing questions. In *The Gifts of Imperfection*, Brené Brown explains that guarding our hearts may be a completely justified and natural response to threats, but it keeps us from knowing and being known. She writes,

> We cultivate love when we allow our most vulnerable and powerful selves to be deeply seen and known, and when we honor the spiritual connection that grows from that offering with trust, respect, kindness, and affection. Love is not something we give or get; it is something that we nurture and grow, a connection that can only be cultivated between two people when it exists within each one of them—we can only love others as much as we love ourselves. Shame, blame, disrespect, betrayal, and the withholding of affection damage the roots from which love grows. Love can only survive these injuries if they are acknowledged, healed, and rare.[1]

I've certainly had to wrestle with my own coping strategies—bringing my deep hurts before the Lord to experience His healing hasn't always been the easiest option. Looking back, I realize I'm who I am today because of the grace of God and because my mother showed me how to navigate life's storms. She taught me that attitude isn't about how we enjoy the good times but how we respond to the struggles, disappointments, detours, shame, and heartache. My mother demonstrated that hardships don't have to define us; instead, we can choose to let them shape us into something stronger, deeper, wiser, and more compassionate.

When my wife, Tonia, and I started our church, God put it on our hearts to create a place for broken, wounded, and hurting people. Most carried wounds from family trauma, but some had been hurt by uncaring people in the churches they'd attended, and coming to us was their way of giving God one more chance. We would invite them to join our church family, and we'd love on them. Some individuals felt our compassion fairly quickly and began their healing journey, while others required more time and interactions to be convinced that we were trustworthy and that our love was genuine. We were in no hurry.

I could tell you story after story of people who experienced the healing love of Jesus and were transformed from the inside out. I was amazed. I had no idea God would entrust so many to our care so we could be a source of healing and hope, just as my mother had been for me. I regularly tell our church, "We're not a hotel for the saint; we're a hospital for the sick."

Please don't misunderstand; this transformative work isn't easy, and it's often quite messy. Broken people aren't like porcelain vases that can be glued back together and look as good as new. People come with all kinds of secret sins and must be convinced that when Jesus said, "It is finished," He meant that He completely paid for all their sins—even *that* one! They come with bitterness, resentment, and self-pity because they've been deeply hurt by someone they trusted. They come with a wagonload of emotional and relational losses that need to be grieved, and grieving is hard work. And they come with a lifetime of self-defeating habits that seldom change overnight. It's a process of introducing them to the Lord's love and teaching them of His faithful presence. In one of David's psalms, he wrote:

> The LORD is near to those who have a broken heart, and saves such as have a contrite spirit.
> —PSALM 34:18

In our church family we've seen God reveal His tenderness and strength to those whose hearts were broken, and we've seen hardened men and women melted by the love of Jesus.

I've seen God do amazing things in my church and community. But some of the biggest moves of God I've witnessed have been in my own family. I've had the tremendous privilege of leading my parents and siblings to Christ. Years ago I was preaching one Sunday morning at a church in Nashville where I was on staff at the time. My topic that morning was one of the plagues in Egypt: "One More Night with the Frogs" (I think you can guess which plague). Moses told Aaron to stretch his rod over the waters, and frogs came out and covered the land. Pharaoh said to Moses, "Entreat the LORD that He may take away the frogs from me and from my people; and I will let the people go, that they may sacrifice to the LORD." Moses asked when he wanted God to remove the frogs, and Pharaoh responded, "Tomorrow" (Exodus 8:8–10). Obviously, the plagues so far weren't bad enough to cause Egypt's ruler to let God's people leave. It took the death of the firstborn sons and livestock before he agreed to free the Israelites. As I preached that morning, I asked, "What will God need to do in your life before you relent and let Him have His way? Don't put it off until tomorrow." When I gave the invitation, my mother stepped into the aisle and came to the altar with tears streaming down her cheeks. I was so thrilled that I kicked my leg as high as it would go and shouted, "That's my mama!" It was the most powerful movement of God I've ever experienced. A few seconds later, my niece, who was on scholarship to play basketball at Belmont University, came forward to receive Christ, and I yelled, "That's my niece!"

Almost a decade later I was the senior pastor at a church in Ashland City, Tennessee. My father had begun attending an Assemblies of God church in town led by a wonderful pastor my father loved—my father's father had been a pastor in that denomination, so Dad felt comfortable attending there. When I became a pastor in the city, Dad started coming to our church.

After attending for some time, he responded to an altar call. As he came forward to give his life to Christ, I had the honor and joy of praying with him. At our church we've watched God touch the lives of addicts, abusers, hopeless people, and arrogant people, as well as rich people, comfortable people, successful people, influential people, and every other branch of humanity with His limitless grace, forgiveness, and power. We've seen broken hearts healed and restored, broken families reunited, and broken dreams redirected. Nothing is impossible with God! When the apostle Paul wrote his first letter to the Corinthians, they were a motley bunch, full of arrogance and division, but Paul pointed them to the wonders of God to give them hope for lasting change. He quoted a passage from Isaiah about the coming glory of God:

> Eye has not seen, nor ear heard, nor have entered into the heart of man the things which God has prepared for those who love Him.
> —1 Corinthians 2:9

Using this passage, Paul was doing surgery on their attitudes, encouraging them to look up and have hope instead of looking down in despair or looking around and seeing others as competition. We face the same challenges.

Let's take a deeper dive into the intricacies of attitude.

What Is Attitude?

Attitude is "a settled way of thinking or feeling about something, a predisposition or tendency to respond positively or negatively toward a specific idea, object, person, or situation."[2] Think of attitude as a filter. Everything we experience—whether positive or negative—passes through this filter before we make sense of it. We can filter out God's truth and love, ending up with cynicism, or we can filter out pessimism and lies, leaving us with faith, hope, and love.

Life doesn't always go the way we expect. Unexpected challenges may *shake* us, but they also have the power to *shape* us—often in extraordinary ways we never imagined. In the Old Testament, Joseph was his father's favorite, living a life of privilege until everything fell apart. His jealous brothers sold him into slavery in Egypt, his master's wife falsely accused him of sexual assault, and he was thrown into prison, where he was seemingly forgotten. His story could have ended in despair. But instead, God was at work behind the scenes, using every setback to position him for something greater. Joseph remained faithful and eventually rose to power in Egypt, saving countless lives, including his own family. While not all our stories will turn out like his, his journey reminds us that even when we can't see the bigger picture, God is still moving.

The same kind of resilience is seen in Viktor Frankl, a Jewish psychiatrist and neurologist who was imprisoned in several Nazi concentration camps during World War II, including Auschwitz and Dachau. He was stripped of everything—his clothes, his name, his dignity—and reduced to a number. He lost his pregnant wife, his parents, and his brother in the camps, never knowing what became of them until after the war. Every day, he faced unimaginable suffering: starvation, hard labor, violence, and the constant presence of death. He saw fellow prisoners give up hope and wither away. His life's work, a manuscript he had hidden in his coat, was taken and destroyed upon arrival. Yet in the midst of all this horror, Frankl discovered something powerful—that even in suffering we can choose our response.

ATTITUDE IS A CHOICE

Both Joseph and Frankl languished in prison as victims of prolonged injustice, but neither of them gave up hope. Their stories remind us that our perspective in tough times can transform our future. Even in his lowest moments, Joseph never lost his faith. Sitting in that dark prison, he didn't give up—he used his God-given gift of interpreting dreams, and that very gift opened the door to his future. His attitude in adversity changed everything.

Similarly, Frankl's most famous quote says, "Everything can be taken from a man but one thing: the last of the human freedoms—to choose one's attitude in any given set of circumstances, to choose one's own way."[3]

One of the most empowering truths about attitude is that it's a *choice*. Many people believe that external circumstances determine their attitude, but that's simply not true. You may not be able to control what happens to you, but you can *always* control how you respond. I often tell my staff, "Life happens to all of us, but how you respond is your responsibility." The concept of personal responsibility is crucial to grasping the impact of attitude.

Your attitude is one of the most powerful tools you possess. It shapes how you experience life, influences your relationships, and determines how you handle challenges. While you can't control everything that happens to you, you can always control your attitude.

Despite experiencing verbal and emotional abuse, my mother chose to live with an abundance of love and hope. She refused to let hardship make her bitter. She helped me learn that our attitude in tough times isn't just about surviving—it's about shaping the life we want to live and the legacy we leave behind.

Tim Keller observed, "Our sadness makes him sad; our pain brings him pain."⁵

Those who feel betrayed need to remember that Jesus was betrayed by Judas and denied by Peter, and all but John ran and hid when He was arrested. Those who have been abused need to remember that Jesus suffered verbal abuse from the religious leaders and physical torture at the hands of the Romans. Those who feel abandoned need to remember that for our sake, the Father abandoned Jesus on the cross so He could pay the penalty for our sins. When we suffer in any way, Jesus doesn't hide His face, laugh, or mock. When we cry, He cries. When we're outraged at injustice, He's even more outraged because He has identified Himself so closely with us.

Do all these circumstances have the ability to affect our attitudes? Oh, yeah! But what's the reason we're tempted to fall into a sour attitude instead of a peaceful one? It's when we allow our circumstances to leave us feeling insecure, abandoned, or belittled. Instead, we need to remember:

- When we *feel* insecure, we *belong* to God, and He holds us in His loving hand.
- When we *feel* abandoned, we *belong* to God, and His face shines on us all the time.
- When we *feel* belittled, we *belong* to God, and we're more valuable to Him than all the world's jewels, gold, and silver.

As much as we try to hide our insecurity with bravado or earn approval by pleasing people, sooner or later we realize it's a losing game. Jesus was secure in His Father's love. When He came out of the waters of baptism, the Holy Spirit descended like a dove, and a voice spoke from heaven: "This is My beloved Son, in whom I am well pleased" (Matthew 3:16–17). As we grow in our experience of being God's beloved son or daughter, cynicism will turn to optimism, a critical spirit to an affirming heart, and a scowl to a smile.

All around us, we see people react to difficulties with sour, selfish attitudes. Our culture doesn't expect people to enjoy peace in the midst of chaos. That's an unexpected result, one that's ours as we find Jesus faithful. If we look at American history and the current economic status of other countries, we see that we live in the most affluent, comfortable culture the world has ever known. But all of us hit snags from time to time. Expectations that are too high and unrealistic inevitably produce bad attitudes, but the experience of God's unending love, wisdom, and power gives us the strength to handle small bumps and tragic heartaches.

Isn't that what you long for? Isn't that the kind of effect you want to have on the people around you? Sure, it is. That's why you picked up this book.

You have the power to manage your attitude.

At the end of each chapter, you'll find some questions to stimulate reflection and provide great discussions for couples and groups. Don't hurry through these—there are no bonus points for speed! As you begin each time, ask God to give you insight, wisdom, and courage to take the steps He directs.

Chapter 2

WHEN LIFE IS UNFAIR

*Surely I have cleansed my heart in vain,
and washed my hands in innocence.
For all day long I have been plagued,
and chastened every morning.*
—Psalm 73:13-14

I wondered why I got such a raw deal. Why did I have to grow up in such a dysfunctional family when I didn't have a choice? Why did my father become an alcoholic? Why was he so cruel to my mother? Why was our family so poor?

Wouldn't you think that since my father grew up with his dad serving as a pastor, he would have gotten the love and guidance he needed? But my dad told stories about his father breaking a switch off a bush in the yard and beating him "until the blood ran down his legs." That wasn't my experience with my dad's dad. I wasn't around him much, but I recall him and my grandmother praying in their living room with the windows open, and people in the neighborhood overhearing them asking God to bless them.

My cousin, a pastor on the coast of Oregon, told me about a story he'd heard about my grandfather. My grandfather spent his life balancing two callings: working for the railroad during the week and serving as a pastor at his church on the weekends. He was dependable and grounded, not the kind of man to chase strange stories. But there was one moment my grandfather talked about that stayed etched in his memory forever.

He was sitting at a red light when he looked over and saw a man in the passenger seat of his car. The man's eyes were sharp, almost otherworldly—like they could see straight through him. Then the man began to speak. He told my grandfather things no stranger could have known and then spoke of what was to come—how he'd lay hands on the sick and they'd be healed and how he'd step into a deeper, more powerful part of his calling.

When he got home, he was in tears. My grandmother found him that way and asked what had happened. He told her everything, and he didn't doubt it for a second—he believed he'd encountered an angel. That moment left a mark on him; he was no longer the same man. He carried himself differently—more sure, more spiritually awake. Whatever was spoken at that stoplight took root and changed the way he lived.

If my father's childhood accounts are true, then clearly my grandfather's transformative experience hadn't given him expert parenting skills, at least not when my dad was a boy.

The Urge to Complain

When life doesn't go our way, our instinctive reaction is to complain and blame someone else. Complaining allows us to vent our frustrations (which can be helpful), but it often reinforces our victim mentality (which is never productive). We ask, "Why?"—and we keep asking, even when there are no answers. Among many other questions, we might ask:

"Why did I lose my job?"

"Why didn't God come through for my family when it felt like we needed Him most?"

"Why did I get cancer?"

"Why can't I get beyond this problem?"

"Why is my daughter throwing her life away on him?"

"Why does my spouse seem so distant?"

THE TEMPTATION TO BLAME

God has put a powerful sense of justice in the heart of every person on earth. We intuitively sense the way things ought to be, and when they go haywire, we conclude that someone is surely to blame. There are actually two very opposite reactions: Some of us are "blame throwers," who assign blame to anyone but ourselves. Others might have some responsibility, but truthfully, we may have been the cause of the problem and are unwilling to admit it. Others of us are "blame sponges," soaking up the blame, whether we're responsible or not. We might wonder why someone would be so overly responsible. One answer is that speaking the truth about another person's responsibility can sometimes be too dangerous, risking fierce blowback. Another could be that we know the other person won't accept responsibility for their actions, so to bring peace, we assume the blame.

Assigning appropriate responsibility isn't always the easiest thing to do. Occasionally, the issue is black and white, but more often both parties are in the gray, sharing at least some of the blame, even if one or both refuse to admit it.

I had every reason to blame my dad for the heartache he caused me, my mom, and my siblings. I could have curled up in a self-protective ball, lashed out at everyone to dominate them, or tried to prove I'm somebody through my achievements. Or I could accept the grace of God, experience His healing touch in the depths of my heart, and choose to break the generational cycle by loving the people God has put in my life.

"Why Me?"

We're observant. We notice when we're up and others are down, and we notice even more when they're up and we're down. When we see others flourish—get a better job, a healthier relationship, more recognition, and better breaks—we think, "That's not fair!" Comparison is a trap. It leads to either superiority or inferiority, blinding us to God's purposes in every detail of our lives.

Social media amplifies the temptation to engage in comparison. We can scroll through posts of dream vacations, perfect dates, tables of delectable dishes, and big wins, with the harsh dose of reality that our lives look exceedingly dull next to all that.

The psalmist Asaph was fuming from this very comparison. He had tried his hardest to walk with God, obey the Scriptures, and live faithfully, but when he looked around, he saw godless people enjoying more success and pleasure than he did. He didn't just glance at them and move on; he was obsessed with them:

- They were strong.
- They had easy lives.
- They were arrogant—and proud of it.

- They got away with violence against people like him.
- They had more than they ever needed.
- They scoffed at "the little people."
- They bragged that they didn't need God at all.
- They claimed God didn't know or didn't care.
- They relished their power, pleasure, and abundance.

When Asaph looked at those people—and kept looking at them—he believed God had let him down. He wrote,

> Surely I have cleansed my heart *in* vain, and washed my hands in innocence. For all day long I have been plagued, and chastened every morning.
> —Psalm 73:13–14

Have you ever felt like that? I have! Comparison may seem natural and normal, but it's actually poison to the soul. We may begin with an accurate assumption: Sometimes life isn't fair. But then we take the next step into unbelief and accusation: God isn't fair! In one of the most vulnerable and honest confessions in the Bible, Asaph shares:

> Thus my heart was grieved, and I was vexed in my mind. I was so foolish and ignorant; I was like a beast before You.
> —Psalm 73:21–22

How does a trapped wild animal react? With desperate fury, twisting this way and that but only growing exhausted and more upset. That's Asaph's description of his condition when he fell short in his comparison to wealthy unbelievers. In one of the most tender passages in the Bible, he tells us how God met him there:

> Nevertheless I am continually with You; You hold me by my right hand. You will guide me with Your counsel, and afterward receive me to glory. Whom have I in heaven but You? And there is none upon earth that I desire besides You. My flesh and my heart fail; but God is the strength of my heart and my portion forever.
> —PSALM 73:23–26

In other words, when Asaph was at his worst, God gently but firmly took him by the hand to teach, guide, and comfort him. The psalmist was so overwhelmed with God's kindness that he realized *nothing* compares to His love and strength.

Have you been there? I have.

"SO, WHAT'S RIGHT?"

Paul picks up this theme in his letter to the Galatians. He and Barnabas had traveled there to share the good news on their first journey. Not long after they left, some religious leaders came from Jerusalem and undercut Paul's teaching that Gentiles were completely accepted into God's family by grace. These intruders taught that Gentiles had to become fully Jewish to become Christians. As you might imagine, this set up a two-tiered community: the "righteous" ones who followed Jewish law to the letter, and the "second string" who trusted only in God's grace. Paul spent the entire letter setting the first group straight. Near the end he addressed the issue of comparison and pride:

> Bear one another's burdens, and so fulfill the law of Christ. For if anyone thinks himself to be something, when he is

nothing, he deceives himself. But let each one examine his own work, and then he will have rejoicing in himself alone, and not in another. For each one shall bear his own load.
—Galatians 6:2–5

To bear someone's burden is the image of someone being trapped under a heavy load they can't lift on their own. They need someone to care enough to help them lift it. The load might be psychological guilt and shame, a health problem, financial distress, fractures in relationships, or other crushing difficulties. However, Paul's main point is to avoid letting pride dictate how we interact with others. We're all sinners saved by grace, and we're all responsible to walk with God in truth, honor, and strength. People with this perspective don't compare their situation with others, either favorably or unfavorably. Their identity and security are formed by the truth that in Christ they're completely loved, forgiven, and accepted, and they're children of the King. This insight dissolves any need to compare or compete with anyone about anything.

In his letter to the Philippians, Paul turns comparison completely upside down. Instead of competing with one another, the love of God and the power of the Spirit enable us to serve one another. Humility, not pride, is the mark of spiritual maturity. He wrote:

> Therefore if there is any consolation in Christ, if any comfort of love, if any fellowship of the Spirit, if any affection and mercy, fulfill my joy by being like-minded, having the same love, being of one accord, of one mind. Let nothing be done through selfish ambition or conceit, but in lowliness of mind let each esteem others better than himself. Let each of you look out not only for his own interests, but also for the

interests of others. Let this mind be in you which was also in Christ Jesus.

—Philippians 2:1–5

Don't misunderstand, in Greek, the language of the New Testament, "if" clauses can have different meanings. Sometimes they are conditional, the way we normally use them—"If it rains tomorrow, we won't have a picnic." But here they are not conditional; they are certain: "If (and it's absolutely true) there is comfort and consolation in Christ… If (and it's absolutely true) we have comfort, the presence of the Spirit, and affection and mercy," then we stand on the solid rock of God's love. Since all this is certain, there's no reason in the world to compare and compete. Instead, we serve one another, rather than trying to gain the upper hand over them.

Paul then quotes what is probably an early hymn about the humility, sacrifice, and glory of Jesus. If He would do that for us, our hearts would be full of gratitude. Paul concludes:

> Do all things without complaining and disputing, that you may become blameless and harmless, children of God without fault in the midst of a crooked and perverse generation, among whom you shine as lights in the world, holding fast the word of life, so that I may rejoice in the day of Christ that I have not run in vain or labored in vain.
>
> —Philippians 2:14–18

Let me paraphrase: Everybody around you is blaming and arguing because they feel cheated, but you, my friend, haven't been cheated. You've been given the greatest gift of all—Jesus Himself! Paul often used the phrase "in Christ" as shorthand to explain our identity as children of God. You are in Christ in His crucifixion, so His sacrificial death is credited to you;

you are in Christ in His perfect life, so His righteousness is credited to you; and you are in Christ in His resurrection, so His new, powerful, God-drenched life is credited to you. That's why you praise God instead of complaining, and that's how you shine like lights instead of adding to the darkness of comparison, despair, and resentment.

What Now?

What needs to happen in our minds and hearts so we aren't knocked around by comparison and competition? The following five principles will help us:

1. We need to realize that life is often unfair.

There, I said it. If we expect everything to go the way we hope, we'll be disappointed quite often. We are flawed people living in a flawed world. Modern technology, medicine, and engineering have made our lives far easier and more comfortable than just a generation or two ago, but these advances have also heightened our expectations of how life should work. We need to recalibrate so we aren't surprised when things don't go as planned.

2. We need to be honest about our reactions.

The Spirit of God wants to pull back the curtain on our attitudes and reveal our self-pity, blame shifting, incessant complaining, and denial that we have a problem with any of these things. When we look at passages of Scripture like the ones we've seen in this chapter, we'll be more realistic about our problems and more grateful for God's grace.

3. We need to embrace God's hidden purposes.

One pastor commented that we know only "a billionth" of what God is up to. That's a very helpful (and humbling) insight.

If God is infinite—and He is—we shouldn't expect to have the inside scoop on everything He's up to. God spoke through Isaiah:

> "For My thoughts *are* not your thoughts, nor are your ways My ways," says the LORD. "For as the heavens are higher than the earth, so are My ways higher than your ways, and My thoughts than your thoughts."
> —Isaiah 55:8–9

We can trust that God is just. While life can be confusing, frustrating, and seemingly absurd, we can cling to the truth that God is the supreme judge, and He is faithful and true. In the second of Paul's recorded letters to the Corinthians, he begins by sharing his deeply painful experiences—which were so bad that he thought he was going to die. With that background everything in the letter takes on an eternal perspective. He describes his suffering:

> But we have this treasure in earthen vessels, that the excellence of the power may be of God and not of us. We are hard-pressed on every side, yet not crushed; we are perplexed, but not in despair; persecuted, but not forsaken; struck down, but not destroyed—always carrying about in the body the dying of the Lord Jesus, that the life of Jesus also may be manifested in our body.
> —2 Corinthians 4:7–10

Paul leaned in to God, trusting that God was doing far more than what he could see. He encouraged them (and us) to hold tight to what we trust but can't yet see:

> Therefore we do not lose heart. Even though our outward man is perishing, yet the inward man is being renewed day by day. For our light affliction, which is but for a moment,

is working for us a far more exceeding and eternal weight of glory, while we do not look at the things which are seen, but at the things which are not seen. For the things which are seen are temporary, but the things which are not seen are eternal.

—2 Corinthians 4:16–18

When you think about giving up, be assured that God is at work behind the scenes.

4. We need to focus on Jesus.

The disciples were often confused. When Jesus performed miracles, they expected the masses to trust in Him and follow Him with all their hearts. It didn't happen that way. At one point in John's account Jesus fed the five thousand (which, counting women and children, was probably closer to twenty thousand). After that He sent the disciples across the lake to the other side. When a storm blew up in the night and they struggled to reach land, Jesus appeared to them walking on the water.

The next day, when they reached shore, they found that many people had walked around the lake to see Jesus again. What did they want? Did they fall down and worship Him as Savior and King? No—they asked Him to open the bakery and give them more bread! What follows is one of the tense conversations Jesus had with people who wanted to follow Him for the wrong reasons. They wanted bread; He offered Himself—the Bread of Life. They refused, and when He didn't repeat the earlier miracle, they walked away. They were focused more on what Jesus could do *for them* than they were on *Jesus Himself.*

The only ones left were the disciples. Jesus didn't go into a frenzy to try to get the others to come back, and He didn't beg the disciples to stay. Instead, He asked, "Do you also want to go away?"

Peter, the common spokesman for the group, answered, "Lord, to whom shall we go? You have the words of eternal life" (John 6:67–68).

There may have already been times in your life (that time may be today), and there will almost certainly be hard times in the future, when you're tempted to walk away from God because He hasn't come through as you hoped. In those pivotal moments keep your eyes on the only One who is eminently trustworthy—Jesus.

FINDING PURPOSE IN YOUR PAIN

One of the most powerful ways to manage your attitude when life feels unfair is to find purpose in your pain. The apostle Paul, who faced immense suffering and persecution, understood this principle. Paul's second letter to the Corinthians begins with despair and the prospect of death, and near the end he describes another problem that plagued him: a "thorn in his flesh" that tormented him. We don't know what it was, but it was bad enough that he wanted it gone! He wrote:

> Concerning this thing I pleaded with the Lord three times that it might depart from me. And He said to me, "My grace is sufficient for you, for My strength is made perfect in weakness." Therefore most gladly I will rather boast in my infirmities, that the power of Christ may rest upon me. Therefore I take pleasure in infirmities, in reproaches, in needs, in persecutions, in distresses, for Christ's sake. For when I am weak, then I am strong.
> —2 CORINTHIANS 12:8–10

Paul was certain that his biggest struggles would someday produce his greatest strengths.

Few stories capture the struggle to believe God in the middle of disaster better than Job's. He had everything—wealth, family, and a life of integrity—until suddenly he lost it all. His children were taken, his health failed, and his possessions disappeared. Anyone in his shoes would have questioned everything, but Job held on. In his pain he declared,

> Naked I came from my mother's womb, and naked shall I return there. The LORD gave, and the LORD has taken away; blessed be the name of the LORD.
> —JOB 1:21

That wasn't blind resignation—it was deep trust. He believed that even when life didn't make sense, God still had a greater purpose. Job also didn't have much encouragement. His wife told him to "curse God and die," and his "friends" kept insisting that the calamities were surely his fault and he needed to expose and confess his sin. Through it all Job kept pursuing God. His story reminds us that faith isn't about having all the answers; it's about trusting even when we don't.

That kind of unwavering trust is also exemplified by Corrie ten Boom, a woman whose courage and compassion remained steadfast in the face of unthinkable injustice. During World War II, she and her family risked their lives to hide Jewish refugees from the Nazis. They were caught, and she and her sister Betsy were sent to Ravensbrück concentration camp. They suffered cruelty, imprisonment, and starvation. Betsy died there, yet Corrie refused to let bitterness take root. Instead, she chose love. She chose forgiveness.

The Shift That Changes Everything

She chose hope. Even in the darkest moments she believed kindness could outshine evil. As she spoke at a church after the war, one of the guards from the camp walked in. When Corrie saw him, she had flashbacks of the brutality he had inflicted. But here he was, seeking God. He reached out his hand to shake hers. She recalls:

> Even as the angry, vengeful thoughts boiled through me, I saw the sin of them. Jesus Christ had died for this man; was I going to ask for more? *Lord Jesus*, I prayed, *forgive me and help me to forgive him....Jesus, I cannot forgive him. Give me Your forgiveness....* And so I discovered that it is not on our forgiveness any more than on our goodness that the world's healing hinges, but on His. When He tells us to love our enemies, He gives along with the command, the love itself.[6]

During the war, Corrie quietly moved through her home, caring for the Jews and knowing that each decision she made could cost her everything—yet choosing to act anyway. Every life she saved was a testament to her unwavering conviction that love is stronger than fear. Even after experiencing betrayal and loss, she continued to share a message of hope and healing.

Paul, Job, and Corrie ten Boom show us that life won't always be fair, but how we respond makes all the difference. Their stories remind us that in times of deep pain, we can either let hardship define us or use it to strengthen our faith and refine our character. Even when we don't understand *why*, we can choose to trust, love, and be a light for others.

The story of the Bible is in four parts: creation, the fall into sin, redemption, and restoration. The first two chapters of Genesis tell us that God created the universe, with earth as the place where heaven and earth met. The third chapter describes our ancestors' rebellion against God, and from there to almost the end of Revelation is the magnificent story of redemption, first pointing to the Messiah who was to come and then showing us the wonder of the Messiah's sacrifice to rescue us from sin and eternal death. But there's one more chapter: restoration. Someday in the new heaven and new earth God will make all things right. Justice will prevail, and there will be no more tears.

After the turning point in *The Lord of the Rings*, Sam Gamgee finds out that his friend Gandalf isn't dead. He's thrilled! And the conversation that follows has stuck with me:

> "I thought you were dead! But then I thought I was dead myself. Is everything sad going to come untrue?" "A great Shadow has departed," said Gandalf, and then he laughed and the sound was like music, or like water in a parched land; and as he listened the thought came to Sam that he had not heard laughter, the pure sound of merriment, for days upon days without count.[7]

The promise of the Bible is that what Sam anticipated, and Gandalf described, will be our reality—probably not today, and maybe not tomorrow, but we can be sure that in the future we will have no reason to wonder if life is unfair or if God is just.

There's one more example we need to learn from. If there has ever been anyone who could say life isn't fair, it's Jesus. No one has ever been more honest, compassionate, tender, joyful, attentive, and righteous, yet He was misunderstood by His friends and despised by religious leaders. In the ultimate expression of love, He suffered the cruelest injustice—crucified on a Roman cross used only for the worst criminals.

The Shift That Changes Everything

He endured excruciating injustice, not to prove He was tough but to prove His love for you and me. Think about that the next time life doesn't seem fair.

Consider this:

1. What are some experiences that cause people to assume life isn't fair?

2. When have you felt that way? How did you think, feel, and act?

3. Look back at Asaph's resentment in Psalm 73 that others had it better than he did. What are ways comparison can eat us alive?

4. Look at how God met Asaph when he was at his worst. What does this tender moment say about God?

5. Put these two passages into your own words:
    2 Corinthians 4:7–10
    2 Corinthians 4:16–18

6. On a scale of 0 (not in the least) to 10 (completely), how well are you living by the five principles described in this chapter?
    I realize that life often isn't fair. _____
    I am honest about my reactions. _____
    I embrace God's hidden purposes. _____
    I trust that God is just. _____
    I focus on Jesus. _____

What do your answers tell you about what you need to work on?

What difference do you think it will make?

> "EVEN WHEN WE DON'T UNDERSTAND WHY, WE CAN CHOOSE TO TRUST, LOVE, AND BE A LIGHT FOR OTHERS."

CHAPTER 3

THE ILLUSION OF CONTROL

*Why do you say, O Jacob,
and speak, O Israel:
"My way is hidden from the LORD,
and my just claim is passed over by my God"?*
—ISAIAH 40:27

Years ago psychologist Ellen Langer observed that many people overestimate their ability to control people and events, even when the outcome is obviously outside their influence. Optimism and confidence are highly positive traits, but they can be taken too far. When people under this illusion fail to orchestrate the results they imagined, they become unnecessarily frustrated, confused, and angry. Those who demand control of every situation can't relax and are only happy if everything goes perfectly, to which I'd say, "Good luck with that!"

We like to think we're in control of our lives. We make plans, set goals, and work hard to achieve them, but wise people recognize there are limits to our ability to control outcomes. No matter how diligent we are, some factors remain outside our grasp. The book of Proverbs gives us the right perspective so we don't fall into the ditch of too much control on one side or the ditch of fatalism and passivity on the other. For instance, Solomon gives clear instructions about the importance of planning:

- "The plans of the diligent lead surely to plenty, but those of everyone who is hasty, surely to poverty" (Proverbs 21:5).
- "The wisdom of the prudent is to understand his way, but the folly of fools is deceit" (Proverbs 14:8).
- "Without counsel, plans go awry, but in the multitude of counselors they are established" (Proverbs 15:22).

Still, even the best plans can hit dead ends and detours. Solomon gives us advice and comfort when this happens:

- "A man's heart plans his way, but the LORD directs his steps" (Proverbs 16:9).
- "Trust in the LORD with all your heart, and lean not on your own understanding; in all your ways acknowledge Him, and He shall direct your paths" (Proverbs 3:5–6).

Fear and Pride

The problem with the illusion of control isn't primarily about the object of our control; it's about our fear or pride (or both). I've talked with people whose chaotic home lives drove them to try to control everything and everyone. They lived in fear that if they relaxed, things would go haywire again, and they couldn't let that happen! But it's not just "those things" that will be out of control; they're afraid that if they take their hands off, *they'll* come unglued!

Kimberly grew up with a demanding mother and a passive dad. She couldn't do enough to please her mom, even though she lived every moment for her approval. When she was a child, Kimberly developed obsessive-compulsive disorder (OCD). She spent every day looking for things she could control—not stepping on seams in the sidewalk, counting the dots in the ceiling tiles (and counting them again the next day and the next), sharpening her pencils over and over again, and many other behaviors to bring order into the disorder of her world.

Other people believe life will go better for everybody if they'd move out of the way and let them make all the decisions. They're brimming with confidence—some would call it arrogance. I knew a businessman who was hired as the CEO of a national company because he excelled at his previous role in another industry. He's a type A, hard-charging, make-it-happen kind of guy. In the first meeting with his direct reports he made it clear that all major decisions were his to make, and if they wondered whether a decision was major, it was. At first, people under him were impressed with his take-charge leadership model, but they soon felt marginalized because they had become mere pawns in his chess game. He didn't value their contributions, nor did he respect them as individuals. Everything revolved around him. But when there were bumps in the road, he was quick to blame someone. It didn't seem to matter who it was, as long as it wasn't him. He took all the responsibility for success and none for any failures. The team spirit that had been present before he arrived dissolved, as people spent much of their time figuring out how to shift blame to others on the team instead of collaborating and encouraging one another. His hyper control raised the stress level for everyone around him, and turnover became a big problem for the top level of the company. Eventually, his constant intensity caused problems for him as well. He developed severe gastrointestinal problems, which only made him more irritable and demanding.

You might say, "Well, Pastor Ted, those both sound like extreme examples." I'd respond, "They're more common in families and the workplace than you might think."

In marriages, couples are initially intrigued by the fact that their spouse is different from them. Opposites attract, you know. But the early impressions of "He takes care of me" sometimes morph into "He always dominates me!" There's a difference! I've spoken to couples who live with enormous tension because one or the other insists on complete control over finances, planning weekly activities, vacations, how to load the dishwasher, and every other aspect of family life. When the other spouse tries to push back, the controlling one barks, "I'm handling all this. Don't you trust me?"

The answer should be: "Trust evaporates in the absence of respect."

And then there's parenting. I'm sure there are some couples who are on the same page throughout the time they raised their children, but I haven't met any of them. Quite often one is stricter and the other more lenient, which causes stress in marriage and becomes a game for the kids to play, pitting one parent against the other. Every stage of child development is challenging, but perhaps none more than adolescence. This period tests the kids *and* the parents. Teens are in the important and necessary process of becoming more independent. Psychologists call it *individuation*, which means the child is carving out an identity apart from his or her parents. For a few kids and their parents, it's a seamless process, but for the vast majority, this season is awkward, confusing, tense, and messy. High-control parents claim they want to protect their children, but they may not provide them with the freedom to grow through trial and error. Of course, some errors can be devastating, so open communication is vital to warn kids of potential harm. However, overcontrol shuts down conversation (at least on one side) and makes the adolescent either angry and rebellious or cave in and complain—neither of which produces a wise, stable, mature young adult.

Let me add that parents can't guarantee that their children will become paragons of virtue. I've known some wonderful, godly, wise, loving parents whose kids went off the rails, and I've known kids from horrible home environments who have learned life's most important lessons and become wonderful spouses and parents.

Every endeavor and every relationship is on the continuum between closed-fisted control and openhanded letting go, and we must shift one way or the other (but probably not to the extremes) depending on the circumstances. For instance, we need to be much more controlling of the environment of a three-year-old than of a son or daughter who has recently married. I've known parents who, it seems, haven't read the passage in Genesis about couples leaving their fathers and mothers and cleaving to one another. These parents treat their grown kids as if they're still in junior high!

We can't control the weather, but we can prepare for whatever comes our way outside. We can't control the economy, but we can follow the principles of good stewardship in earning, saving, spending, and giving. We can't control our bosses, but we can live responsibly and communicate clearly. But some of us spend an enormous amount of mental and emotional energy trying to control (or being upset that we can't control) the uncontrollable. We often live with a false sense of power, and when life intervenes, we feel overwhelmed.

What You Can Control

While there are many things beyond our control, there are areas where we have influence and responsibility. The key is learning to focus on these areas rather than getting caught up in things we can't change. So, what *can* you control?

1. Your Attitude

Your attitude sets the tone for your entire life. Philippians 4:8 tells us to focus our minds on things that are true, noble, right, pure, lovely, admirable, excellent, and praiseworthy. This isn't just a suggestion; it's a powerful strategy for maintaining a positive attitude. You have a choice—choose to trust God.

2. Your Actions

While you can't control the outcome of every situation, you *can* control your actions. For example, if you lose your job, you can't control the job market, but you can control how actively you search for new opportunities, how you present yourself to potential employers, and how you use your time during unemployment. Colossians 3:23 (NIV) encourages us to "work at it with all your heart, as working for the Lord, not for human masters." This verse reminds us that our efforts matter, regardless of the situation. We're called to do our best in whatever we do, trusting that God will handle the results.

3. Your Reactions to Others

You can't control how other people behave, but you can control your reactions to them. If someone is rude, unkind, or thoughtless, you have the power to choose how you respond. Romans 12:17–18 (NIV) says, "Do not repay anyone evil for evil. Be careful to do what is right in the eyes of everyone. If it is possible, as far as it depends on you, live at peace with everyone." While you can't control other people's actions, you can do your part to live in peace with those around you by choosing thoughtful, mature, constructive responses.

4. Your Responsibilities

Engineers are trained and temperamentally wired to work at the control end of the continuum, and I'm glad, because I don't want buildings or bridges to fall around me! And who would want an air traffic controller who is on the lenient end of the continuum? Most of us don't have responsibilities that could harm others if we're not faithful, so it's our task to determine our limits in each role and relationship. Our primary role is to be faithful to God's calling, and our primary impact on people is to love them the way Jesus loves. Not sure what that looks like? During the days between Palm Sunday and Good Friday, Jesus was in Jerusalem teaching about the kingdom. John puts us in the moment:

> Now before the Feast of the Passover, when Jesus knew that His hour had come that He should depart from this world

> to the Father, having loved His own who were in the world, He loved them to the end.
> —John 13:1

We might think the Greek word for "the end" refers to the end of time. It's certainly that, but it's more. It means He loved them (and us) to the fullest extent, the uttermost, demonstrated by the supreme sacrifice on the cross. How do we love one another? Paul pointed back to the cross and our new status in God's family, and then he pointed us to follow Jesus' example of love:

> Therefore, as the elect of God, holy and beloved, put on tender mercies, kindness, humility, meekness, longsuffering; bearing with one another, and forgiving one another, if anyone has a complaint against another; even as Christ forgave you, so you also must do. But above all these things put on love, which is the bond of perfection.
> —Colossians 3:12–14

Letting Go

When I think about what I need to hold on to and what I need to let go of, I run it through a mental grid and consider several factors: Do I have the time to do it? Is it my God-given calling and responsibility, or is it an add-on? Do I have the talents and gifts to pull it off? And is someone else better positioned to do it? Years ago I piled far too much on my plate. I thought I had to do virtually everything. Why? I told myself it was for the glory of God, but in reality it was out of pride in thinking I could do anything, and fear of what people would think of me if I gave the task to someone else. I've learned that leadership isn't doing everything—it's equipping others to do everything. When Tonia and I started a church with twenty people,

THE ILLUSION OF CONTROL

I did everything from preaching to picking up the trash and even cleaning toilets. There was nothing I wouldn't do. While serving my church family in humility was a wonderful place to start, as we've grown and my responsibilities have increased, I've learned the art and science of delegation. If I micromanage our gifted staff members, I will frustrate them and burn myself out. I need to hire people with skills and a good attitude, equip them, and let them play their vital role in our church and God's kingdom. This insight has focused my attention on what's most important, honored the people around me, and enabled much more growth—personally, in our staff, and in our church.

Letting go of what you can't control is one of the most freeing things you can do for yourself. However, it's also one of the most challenging. We like to believe that if we try hard enough, we can manage every aspect of our lives. The truth, however, is that trying to control the uncontrollable leads to stress, anxiety, and incredible frustration. Letting go isn't passive fatalism. Fatalism is giving up in despair. The kind of letting go I'm describing is opening a clenched fist and putting our worries in the hands of a loving and powerful God. The two are miles apart.

In the summer of 1943, World War II was raging in Europe and the Pacific. At the time, Germany, Italy, and Japan had conquered large parts of the world, and the conflict's outcome was still unknown. Lutheran theologian Reinhold Niebuhr wrote a series of messages to provide perspective for people who lived every day wondering what would happen to their sons in combat. They felt terribly out of control. Niebuhr wrote a prayer as part of his sermon series. We know it as the

Serenity Prayer. Many people know the first part, but all of it is instructive:

> God, give me grace to accept with serenity
>   the things that cannot be changed,
> Courage to change the things
>   which should be changed,
> and the Wisdom to distinguish
>   the one from the other.
> Living one day at a time,
>   Enjoying one moment at a time,
> Accepting hardship as a pathway to peace,
>   Taking, as He did,
> This sinful world as it is,
>   Not as I would have it,
> Trusting that He will make all things right,
>   If I surrender to His will,
> That I may be reasonably happy in this life,
>   And supremely happy with Him forever in the next.
>   Amen.

People in Alcoholics Anonymous have adopted this prayer to help them distinguish between what they can control (their choice to drink) and what they can't control (their urges, the responses of people, etc.). It's a beautiful and powerful prayer for all of us.

Payoffs

Trusting God enough to let go of the things and people we can't control lightens our load and brings several benefits:

The Illusion of Control

- **Reduced Stress and Anxiety**

Many of us have no idea what life can be without the oppressive burden of trying to control every circumstance. Jesus invites us:

> Come to Me, all you who labor and are heavy laden, and I will give you rest. Take My yoke upon you and learn from Me, for I am gentle and lowly in heart, and you will find rest for your souls. For My yoke is easy and My burden is light.
> —Matthew 11:28–30

Take a moment to check in with yourself—is your load light?

- **Increased Peace**

When we expect a pleasant and easy life, we set ourselves up to be rocked when we hit rough patches. Unrealistic expectations inevitably lead to the feeling that we're out of control. We often settle for second-class peace—the temporary absence of hassles—but God's peace is far deeper, richer, and more comprehensive. In an article about sin and grace, seminary president and professor Cornelius Plantinga Jr. observes:

> In the Bible shalom means universal flourishing, wholeness, and delight—a rich state of affairs in which natural needs are satisfied and natural gifts fruitfully employed, a state of affairs that inspires joyful wonder as the creator and savior opens doors and welcomes the creatures in whom he delights. Shalom, in other words, is the way things are supposed to be.[8]

Isn't that what you want? Yeah, me too. That's what Jesus offers. On the night He was betrayed, He stunned the disciples by telling them (again) that He was going away. He promised the Holy Spirit would come to guide and empower them, but they were confused, worried, and feeling out of control. Jesus promised a peace that surpasses understanding:

> Peace I leave with you, My peace I give to you; not as the world gives do I give to you. Let not your heart be troubled, neither let it be afraid.
> —JOHN 14:27

Jesus' peace isn't escape from problems, and it isn't a distraction from worries. It's confidence that when life seems out of control, we can be confident that He knows, He cares, and He's working behind the scenes. We can count on Him.

- **Improved Relationships**

You know it, and I know it: When people feel controlled, they get understandably angry and either push back or get away from us. I think it's safe to say that much of the tension we experience in relationships is caused by too much or too little control. When we trust God enough to relax and truly listen to people, they feel understood and affirmed. Of course, if we've been too controlling for a long time, it will take a while to convince them we've truly changed—but it's a beautiful thing when it happens.

- **More Time and Energy for What Really Matters**

The compulsion to control people and outcomes is exhausting. We invest countless hours thinking, planning, worrying, double-checking, correcting people, and doing it all again the next day. When our hearts are filled with God's peace, our priorities change. We're no longer consumed with the need to manage everyone and everything. We can slow down, love people instead of using them to accomplish our goals, and enjoy God's many blessings.

The Illusion of Control

Letting go of what you can't control is one of the most liberating choices. By focusing on what you can control—your attitude, actions, reactions, and responsibilities—you can navigate life's challenges with confidence, knowing that God is in control of everything else.

In the Gap

Sometimes it's up to us to stand in the gap for others when circumstances feel out of our control. We may need to take bold action, or we may need to pray boldly. Either way, we need courage. After Moses led God's people out of Egypt, they came to the Red Sea. Behind them, Pharaoh's army and chariots were coming fast. To the human eye there seemed to be no way out. But instead of giving in to fear, Moses trusted God. His faith turned an impossible situation into one of the most extraordinary miracles in history—the sea parted, and the people of God walked through on dry ground. His story reminds us that even when the path forward seems blocked, faith can make a way.

Centuries later we see similar courage in Britain's prime minister during World War II, Winston Churchill. By the summer of 1940, Hitler's German army had conquered Poland and then turned on Belgium, Holland, and France. The British and French forces had been cornered on a strip of France near Dunkirk, and a miraculous effort saved hundreds of thousands of men. Only a few miles of water separated the Nazis from England's shores. Some members of the British government feared invasion and occupation, and they advised Churchill to go to Hitler, surrender, and take the best terms he would offer, but Churchill was made of sterner stuff. In one of his most famous speeches in the House of Commons, he announced to the radio audience:

> Even though large tracts of Europe and many old and famous States have fallen or may fall into the grip of the Gestapo and all the odious apparatus of Nazi rule, we shall not flag or fail. We shall go on to the end, we shall fight in France, we shall fight on the seas and oceans, we shall fight with growing confidence and growing strength in the air, we shall defend our Island, whatever the cost may be, we shall fight on the beaches, we shall fight on the landing grounds, we shall fight in the fields and in the streets, we shall fight in the hills; we shall never surrender, and even if, which I do not for a moment believe, this Island or a large part of it were subjugated and starving, then our Empire beyond the seas, armed and guarded by the British Fleet, would carry on the struggle, until, in God's good time, the New World, with all its power and might, steps forth to the rescue and the liberation of the old.[9]

The truth is, we all face moments when we feel powerless and completely out of control. But like Moses and Churchill, we can choose to trust, stand firm, and believe that even in the most chaotic times God is still leading us forward. When we anchor ourselves in faith, we find clarity, strength, and the courage to walk through whatever stands in our way.

EVEN THEN

If you think your life is out of control, look back at the nation of Israel a few hundred years before Christ. The Assyrians crushed the northern kingdom, and years later the Babylonians destroyed Jerusalem and the temple, taking the best and brightest into exile to serve their king. Understandably, God's people felt completely helpless and hopeless, without a hint of control over their lives. Into this mess stepped the prophet Isaiah. He spoke God's promises to comfort the people. The turning point in his account is chapter 40. He reminds the people that God will send His messenger before Him to proclaim His love and power. To those who felt abandoned and beleaguered he announced:

> Behold, the Lord God shall come with a strong hand, and His arm shall rule for Him; behold, His reward is with Him, and His work before Him. He will feed His flock like a shepherd; He will gather the lambs with His arm, and carry them in His bosom, and gently lead those who are with young.
> —Isaiah 40:10–11

Isaiah tells the people they can trust God in the middle of their suffering because He is the creator, far more powerful than any nation (including Babylon) and wiser than any ruler (including the Babylonian king). God's purposes will not be stopped—He will accomplish His will no matter how things look at the moment. The people, though, were complaining that God had hidden His face and wasn't interested in them any longer. Isaiah doesn't let them off the hook. He challenges them:

> Why do you say, O Jacob, and speak, O Israel: "My way is hidden from the Lord, and my just claim is passed over by my God"?
> —Isaiah 40:27

He reminds them of God's character: He's the Creator who knows all things and has compassion for those He loves. He gives power to those who are weak.

THE SHIFT THAT CHANGES EVERYTHING

> But those who wait on the LORD shall renew their strength; they shall mount up with wings like eagles, they shall run and not be weary, they shall walk and not faint.
> —ISAIAH 40:31

When we think of waiting, we usually imagine only the element of time. Waiting on the Lord, though, has a richer, more profound meaning. The waiter at a restaurant is attentive to the guests, noticing what they want or need before being asked. In the same way when we wait on the Lord, we're not just drumming our fingers to kill time before God acts. We're attentive to Him, seeking His face and listening to Him speak to us through the Scriptures, the Spirit's whisper, a wise mentor, or some other means. If we fix our minds and hearts on Him, we'll draw on His strength, comfort, and wisdom.

Notice the progression in this verse in Isaiah. We normally think of walking, then running, and then flying, but it's the opposite here. Sometimes we sense God's presence and power so fully that our hearts soar, most of the time we "run the race" before us with endurance, and occasionally we're so burdened that all we can do is take one more step toward God. All three of these are elements of a life of faith, and all three require a hopeful attitude that God will do what only He can do.

One of life's most important lessons is learning to distinguish between what we can control and what we cannot. Much of our frustration, stress, and anxiety come from trying to manage things that are simply beyond our control. Learning to recognize the boundaries of our influence while letting go of the things we can't change is a key component of maintaining a healthy attitude, especially when life gets difficult, as it was

THE ILLUSION OF CONTROL

for God's people in exile. When they felt out of control, Isaiah reminded them that God is always in control.

Consider this:

1. How would you define and describe "the illusion of control"?

2. How does pride feed that illusion?

3. How does fear prompt it?

4. What are some factors in life within your control? And outside it?

5. Where do you normally fall on the continuum between "obsessive control" and "loose as a goose"? What are the benefits and liabilities of your approach?

6. Which of the payoffs of trust is most attractive to you (reduced stress and anxiety, increased peace, improved relationships, or more time and energy for what really matters)?

7. Look again at Isaiah 40. If you'd been one of the children of Israel after the Babylonians had destroyed Jerusalem, how would you have received Isaiah's message? Look at it again through the lens of your current circumstances. How do you receive it now?

8. Describe times when your heart soared, when you ran with endurance, and when you could barely

take one more step. How did God meet you in each season?

> "LETTING GO OF WHAT YOU CAN'T CONTROL IS ONE OF THE MOST FREEING THINGS YOU CAN DO FOR YOURSELF."

CHAPTER 4

DEALING WITH DIFFICULT PEOPLE

For if you love those who love you, what reward have you? Do not even the tax collectors do the same? And if you greet your brethren only, what do you do more than others? Do not even the tax collectors do so? Therefore you shall be perfect, just as your Father in heaven is perfect.
—MATTHEW 5:46–48

Years ago I was on a break from being a pastor. I had gotten a divorce and left the ministry, and I didn't know if I'd ever be a pastor again. I took a job in Boise, Idaho, as the director of fixed operations at a Hyundai-Nissan dealership, overseeing parts and service. The owner of the company was a first-class micromanager. It wasn't that he insisted on making major decisions; he insisted on making *every* decision! He had exceptionally high standards for me and my department, but he refused to delegate authority, which hindered my success.

The Shift That Changes Everything

During my job application and interview process with him, I was met with a welcoming and pleasant demeanor, which didn't initially suggest the authoritarian leadership style I later saw so clearly. He knew I was a Christian, so he asked me how I'd handle my faith in the workplace. I replied, "If you think I'm going to harass people about my faith, that's not going to happen." I let that sink in for a few seconds and then continued, "Inevitably, some people will ask me why I treat them with kindness and respect, and I'll tell them it's because Jesus has treated me with kindness and respect." He nodded. I guess my answer satisfied him that I wouldn't stand on the hood of a car and preach hellfire and damnation.

It didn't take long for us to clash. The mechanics in our service department were doing a great job, but we had a long backlog of impatient customers. I planned to hire more people, but my boss wouldn't hear it. He was afraid he'd be paying too many salaries if the business slowed down. I tried to explain that we were losing a lot of business because customers didn't want to wait so long for us to service their cars, but he was deaf to my reasoning. Customers were upset, and mechanics were stressed out, but I felt handcuffed. He told me more than once, "You just need to get the job done with the people you already have." It was like Pharaoh telling the Israelites to keep up the exact tally of bricks but without providing straw for them.

After our first conversation—not long after I started working there—I gave him the benefit of the doubt. It was his company, and I was the new guy. But after the third or fourth time I pleaded and reasoned with him about the need for more help, I was frustrated and angry. He was demanding more from my team and me than we could produce. I was optimistic that if we provided outstanding service in a reasonable amount of time, customers would flock to us, and we'd have no trouble keeping everyone busy. He was pessimistic, willing to annoy existing customers and create resentment among the team to save a few dollars.

I'm a producer and a results-oriented guy, and I have experience in leadership and delegation. We weren't getting the outcomes I knew we could produce, which drove me crazy. I was caught between the needs of customers, the stress of our employees, and the owner's stubbornness. I was determined to treat him with respect, but my capacity for patience was running out.

Tonia's cousin planted a church in the area, and I occasionally preached there. It was salve on my wounded soul, and I thought more about my calling. I sensed God leading me back into ministry, but I reminded Him, "Don't you understand? I've been divorced, and the big d-word doesn't work in pastoral ministry."

As I prayed and told God I'd been disqualified, I heard Him say as clearly as any other conversation, "Who told you that?"

I replied, "Well, no one had to tell me. That's just the way it is."

He challenged my assumption: "Son, My calling is irrevocable. You need to return to what *I* have called you to do." That season under the leadership of the dealership owner pressed me to reevaluate what God had called me to do and drove me deeper into His presence so I could hear His voice.

It wasn't long before God opened a door for us to move to Mississippi to plant a church. That was over fourteen years ago, and I've never looked back. My painful experience with the dealership's owner taught me valuable lessons about leadership.

Sometimes God gives us models to emulate, but occasionally He puts us around people who demonstrate what not to do. Both are important classrooms.

All Types

Life is full of family members, friends, coworkers, and neighbors, but not all these relationships are easy. At some point we all encounter difficult people. Whether it's someone at work who constantly criticizes your efforts, a family member who is perpetually negative, or a neighbor who seems to go out of their way to annoy you, dealing with difficult people can be one of the most challenging aspects of life. How we handle these interactions can either improve the situation or exacerbate it.

Experts in relationships have identified various types of individuals who strain our ability to relate to them with honesty and integrity. In other words, they often bring out the worst in us. Your list may be longer or shorter, but this covers most of them:

- **The Know-It-All**

I met a lady once who told me with solemn earnestness that she had all the spiritual gifts, and nothing was beyond her ability. (I wanted to ask if she considered self-reflection and humility as two of her strengths.) People who insist they have all the answers are grandiose, believing they're the smartest people in the room and that everyone else should shut up and let them wax eloquent about every problem and opportunity. When anyone has the boldness to challenge them, they double down, fiercely insisting they're right and that the other person is not just misguided but stupid.

- **The Bully**

Some people position themselves as one up. They have to win at all costs—arguments, decisions, or competitions—and use intimidation to get their way. They require blind loyalty from others, and when they don't get it, they can be cruel by cutting people to shreds. Bullies believe they're being magnanimous by letting underlings follow them. All of us can be demanding at times, but bullies use force repeatedly and intentionally to dominate others.

- **The Victim**

Playing the victim role enables a person to deflect responsibility through complaining, passivity, and blaming others for their problems. They talk about how they've been wronged, and in fact their wounds are central to their identity. Some victims are pitiful and expect others to take care of them, but others demand that somebody step in and make things right for them. Of course, these demands are seldom met, which reinforces their belief that people (and God) have let them down.

- **The Gossip**

When secrets are combined with slander, the information excites those privileged to hear it. It's so much fun to know something others don't even suspect. It's intoxicating, and we can't get enough. Maybe Solomon wrote so much about gossip because he had so many wives. (And while it's true that many women can tend toward gossip more naturally than men, it's still a pitfall men need to watch out for.) Whatever the reason, he's an expert on the topic. He wrote:

> A fool's mouth is his destruction, and his lips are the snare of his soul. The words of a talebearer are like tasty trifles, and they go down into the inmost body.
> —Proverbs 18:7–8

Gossip may start as a seemingly innocent lark, and those involved form their own version of a secret society, but they betray friends and create divisions. What begins as fun ends in cruelty and heartache.

- **The Perfectionist**

We applaud people whose high personal standards drive their pursuit of excellence, but when these standards are carried too far, they become a liability for the person and a thorn for others. Perfectionists are insecure, believing their personal value is tied to their performance, so nothing less than perfection will do. They believe they're the only ones who really care about doing a job well, and they look down on everyone else as lazy and incompetent. Their pursuit of excellence, then, poisons relationships.

- **The People Pleaser**

These people are also insecure, but their coping strategy is quite different from that of the perfectionist. They tie their hope to winning approval, not achieving high performance. They're chameleons, agreeing with the person in front of them but changing colors and tunes when the next person comes along. Bullies read them like a book and manipulate them with a combination of praise (to make them want more) and criticism (to make them comply with demands). They often volunteer to serve more and longer, hoping someone will appreciate them.

- **The Pessimist**

Some people can only see the dark and dangerous side of any proposal. They're sure the worst will happen. As the saying goes, "They can find something wrong with a bowl of ice cream!" They may have been deeply hurt in the past, so they assume nothing good can happen in the future. Or they may have an analytical nature that sees through blind optimism (which is disgusting to them) but struggles to articulate positive steps toward a better outcome. Pessimists are wet blankets on the attitudes of people around them.

Possible Causes

Before exploring strategies for dealing with difficult people, it's helpful to understand why they act the way they do. Annoying, defensive behavior often stems from unresolved hurts, personal insecurities, or other issues. While the cause doesn't excuse bad behavior, it can help you approach the situation with empathy rather than frustration. Here are a few common reasons people act in difficult ways:

1. Insecurity and Low Self-Esteem

Many people are difficult because they feel insecure. They may compensate for these insecurities by being overly critical, controlling, passive, or confrontational. Their negative behavior is often a way of projecting their fears and inadequacies onto others.

2. Present Stress

They may be going through a tough time at home, struggling with financial problems, dealing with a difficult spouse or kids, or facing a health crisis. Or, like my situation at the car dealership, their stress may come from a toxic work environment.

When someone is overwhelmed by their circumstances, they may lash out or behave in ways that seem irrational or unkind.

3. Past Trauma

People who have experienced trauma, abuse, or rejection in the past may develop defense mechanisms to protect themselves from being hurt again. They may be overly guarded, suspicious, eager to please, passive, or quick to anger.

4. Personality Differences

Sometimes people get on our nerves simply because of personality differences. We all have different temperaments, communication styles, and ways of handling conflict. What one person sees as assertiveness, another may interpret as aggression. One person may view herself as careful and thoughtful, while another may see her as overly cautious or indecisive. These differences can easily (and tragically) lead to misunderstandings and tension.

While understanding what's going on "under the hood" of difficult people may not make it easier to deal with them, it enables you to approach the situation with a bit more understanding and compassion. When you recognize that factors outside your control may drive someone's behavior, you're less likely to take it personally and more likely to respond with patience and understanding.

Responding Instead of Reacting

One of the most important principles for dealing with difficult people is learning to respond rather than react. Reacting is often an emotional, knee-jerk response to someone's behavior. When we react, we're likely to say or do something out of frustration or anger, which can escalate the conflict. Responding, on the other hand, is a thoughtful, measured approach that considers the bigger picture.

Proverbs 15:1 (NIV) provides timeless wisdom: "A gentle answer turns away wrath, but a harsh word stirs up anger." Responding with gentleness, even when you're dealing with someone who is difficult, can defuse the situation and prevent it from escalating. Here are a few strategies for responding rather than reacting:

1. Pause before you speak.

When you feel your emotions rising, take a moment before responding. This can be as simple as taking a deep breath or counting to ten. This brief pause allows you to think more clearly and choose a thoughtful response rather than a reactive one.

2. Stay calm.

It can be challenging to remain calm when someone is being difficult, but keeping your emotions in check is key to handling the situation with grace. When we feel threatened—and our sense of composure can feel threatened by all types of difficult people—our immediate reaction is fight or flight. When our adrenaline kicks in, some of us instinctively "bow up" and try to dominate, while others can't stand being in the person's presence and want to run away and hide. When you stay calm, you control your response and prevent the situation from spiraling out of control.

3. Read the room.

In conflict, people may have opposite reactions—and they're often married to each other! Some people "get big"—they sit up, glare, get louder, accuse, and try to intimidate. That's their way to win in the confrontation. Others "get little"—they shrink in their chairs, avoid eye contact, soften their voices to a whisper, apologize even if they did nothing wrong, and wish they could evaporate into the ceiling. That's their way of getting the conflict over as soon as possible. Neither of these adequately addresses the real problem. In fact, they create another layer of problems because they're reinforcing unproductive reactions to tense situations. It's helpful to notice your own reaction so you can choose a different course, and it's also helpful to read the room and notice the reactions of others so you don't get caught up in playing the game of intimidation or passivity.

4. Ask clarifying questions.

Sometimes difficult people act out because they feel misunderstood or unheard. Instead of jumping to conclusions, ask clarifying questions to understand their perspective more accurately. Don't come across as an attorney cross-examining a witness! Sit back, relax, and respectfully ask who, what, when, how, or why—whichever is appropriate. And you can always make the golden statement: "Tell me more about that."

5. Mirror what the person is saying.

One of the most helpful communication techniques is mirroring, which is reflecting back what you hear the person saying. You can say, "I want to make sure I understand you. Here's what I think you're saying..." When you articulate your understanding, the person can respond, "Yes, that's it. Thanks for listening," or, "You got part of it. Let me explain the other part again," or maybe, "No, that's not it. Let me try again." Don't stop until the person is sure he or she has been heard and understood.

6. Take responsibility for your emotions.

While someone else's behavior may be difficult, what you choose to do with your feelings and how you respond to them is ultimately your responsibility. While people's actions toward you may incite feelings of frustration, anger, or hurt, you are ultimately in control of your emotions and what you do with them. By taking responsibility for your feelings, you empower yourself to respond in a way that aligns with your values rather than being driven by the actions of others.

How we treat others—especially those who challenge or hurt us—says a lot about who we are. When conflicts arise, our attitude can either add fuel to the fire or bring peace and healing. It's not an easy choice. Everything in us wants to push back, defend ourselves, and hold on to resentment. But Jesus calls us to something higher. He invites us to see people not as enemies but as individuals in need of grace, just like us.

Over the course of my life, I've had trouble relating to a particular group of people. Their personalities are the polar opposite of mine, so it's hard for me to comprehend their attitudes and behavior. I'm a type A go-getter. I love challenges, and I'm highly motivated to make every moment count. You can probably guess the kind of people who used to drive me crazy—the ones who value relaxing over achieving and are just as happy doing nothing as doing something. In my early years, I didn't try to understand them. I was just convinced they were wrong! Over the years, I've learned that our different personalities don't make one right and the other wrong. Both are created in the image of God, possess incalculable value, and play a vital role in the kingdom of God. I've even learned the value in taking time to rest—allowing the gift of Sabbath to refresh and restore my soul before jumping into the next thing. I wish I could say it was an easy lesson to learn, but it wasn't.

As we've read earlier, Joseph's brothers betrayed him, selling him into slavery and telling their father he was dead. If anyone had a right to hold a grudge, it was him! But when life brought them back together years later, Joseph didn't choose an attitude of revenge; he chose an attitude of forgiveness. Instead of bitterness, he extended grace, and his act of mercy not only restored his family but changed the course of history. When their father, Jacob, died, the brothers were afraid Joseph would take revenge. In terror they fell on their faces and implored him to have mercy. They said, "Behold, we are your servants." The historian takes us to this poignant moment:

> Joseph said to them, "Do not be afraid, for am I in the place of God? But as for you, you meant evil against me; but God meant it for good, in order to bring it about as it is this day, to save many people alive. Now therefore, do not be afraid; I will provide for you and your little ones." And he comforted them and spoke kindly to them.
> —Genesis 50:19–21

Joseph didn't see himself as the judge, jury, and executioner—that's God's job. His brothers had betrayed him, but God gave him an eternal perspective—a bigger view of the situation. God had used the betrayal to orchestrate the elevation of Joseph to the second chair in the kingdom of Egypt, and there he became the administrator who saved the nation and his family from starvation in the famine. His brothers hadn't provided for him, but he chose to forgive and provide for them and their families. It was a remarkable picture of grace in action.

Joseph's story reminds us that forgiveness isn't about excusing what happened; it's about freeing ourselves from the weight of resentment and choosing healing instead. This idea isn't just something we read in Scripture; we see it in history too. Mahatma Gandhi faced hatred and oppression, yet he refused to use violence in his pursuit of justice. Instead, he met hostility with kindness and respect, transforming enemies into allies through his relentless commitment to nonviolence. Imagine Gandhi standing before those who opposed him, not with anger but with steady resolve, offering words of peace where there had been only racism and hate. His example proves that kindness and understanding have the power to reshape even the most hostile situations.

Both Joseph and Gandhi show us that attitudes of love and forgiveness aren't just ideals—they're choices we can make every day. And in a world filled with division, those choices matter more than ever. When we respond with grace to annoying, hostile, demanding people, we don't just change our hearts; we create a ripple effect, inspiring others to do the same.

Setting Boundaries

One of the most important tools for maintaining an attitude of peace while dealing with difficult people is setting healthy boundaries. Boundaries are limits that you set for yourself to protect your emotional, physical, and mental well-being. They help you define what behavior in others is acceptable and what isn't, and they prevent others from taking advantage of you. They require a measure of self-awareness to know how far is too far, and they require courage to state them clearly and enforce the consequences.

Setting boundaries doesn't mean you're being unkind or selfish; rather, it's a way to ensure that your relationships are respectful and healthy. Here are some tips for setting boundaries with difficult people:

1. Be clear and direct.

When setting a boundary, it's important to be clear and direct about what you need. For example, if someone is speaking to you in a disrespectful or hurtful way, you might say, "I'm happy to have a conversation with you, but I need us to speak respectfully to each other. If that doesn't happen, I'll step away from the conversation." Being clear about your expectations helps the other person understand where the line is.

2. Get advice and assistance.

Those who have endured abusive relationships either want to erect a ten-foot-thick concrete wall around themselves or think asking for a drink of water in the desert is too demanding. In other words, people who are most in need of setting effective boundaries often have no clue how to do it. It's wise to find someone who "has been down this road before" to help you. Reading a book on boundaries is also very helpful, but I advise finding a pastor, counselor, personal coach, or support-group sponsor who has experience.

3. Use "I" statements.

When setting boundaries, it's helpful to use "I" statements rather than "you" statements. For example, instead of saying, "You always talk down to me," try saying, "I feel disrespected when we speak like this, and I need us to have a more respectful conversation." This approach helps to reduce defensiveness and focuses on your feelings rather than blaming the other person. A helpful template is to use three "I" statements:

1. "I feel"—"I feel hurt...angry...afraid...confused," or whatever emotion you're feeling.

2. "I want"—My "I want" is always, "I want a relationship based on trust and respect."

3. "I will"—This statement of intent depends on the particular situation and focuses on honesty and accountability. For instance, you might say, "I'm making a commitment to be honest with you when I believe you've lied to me, and I will enforce the consequences I've set."

If the person is abusive, don't use an "I feel" statement because it will make you vulnerable to another attack. Skip to the other two. One more piece of advice: Write out what you plan to say and role-play it with a safe person. When we face the person who has lied to us, betrayed us, or treated us badly, some of us go "mush-brained and jelly-legged." You can avoid this (or at least minimize it) by writing down what you plan to say and practicing it.

Many people believe they can talk long enough and persuasively enough to make a bad person good and an irresponsible person responsible. Don't fall into that trap. Say what you need to say, and end the conversation. Staying too long gives the other person power over you, weakens your position, and opens the door to further damage in the relationship.

4. Enforce the boundary.

Once you've set a boundary, it's important to be consistent in enforcing it. If you allow someone to cross your boundaries without consequence, you're telling them that you're an easy mark, you're weak, and they can treat you with disrespect and get away with it. It may require you to be more courageous than you've ever been, but don't back down. The boundary is good for both of you. It clarifies reality for you so you no longer excuse the inexcusable, and it offers the other person the opportunity to begin to earn trust. Both are essential for strained and broken relationships to be healed.

5. Know when to walk away.

In some cases the best boundary you can set is to remove yourself from the situation altogether. If someone continues to be difficult despite your best efforts to engage respectfully, it may be time to limit or end your interactions with that person. Walking away doesn't mean you're giving up—it means you're prioritizing your well-being. Loving an irresponsible or abusive person means "speaking the truth in love"; however, they may not want to hear the hard truth, even if it's spoken in love. Paul wrote to the Christians in Rome, "Repay no one evil for evil. Have regard for good things in the sight of all men. If it is possible, as much as depends on you, live peaceably with all men" (Romans 12:17–18). Notice, Paul said, "If it is possible," which implies that sometimes it's *not* possible. Physical and psychological distance is often necessary to regain the ability to think clearly. Do what it takes.

One of the most difficult problems people can face is excessive strain in a marriage. They began with high hopes, but for many possible reasons, those hopes were dashed. Many Christian leaders identify two legitimate causes of divorce: adultery and abandonment. Seminary professor and former president of the Evangelical Theological Society Dr. Wayne Grudem held the same position for his entire career until he looked at the historical context of 1 Corinthians 7:15 (ESV), which reads, "But if the unbelieving partner separates, let it be so. In such cases the brother or sister is not enslaved. God has called you to peace."

The clause "in such cases" had been understood to apply only to the immediate context of abandonment, but Grudem studied the phrase in Greek literature of the period and found that it doesn't refer only to the single scenario the writer mentioned but to others that are similar. He wrote, "These examples led me to conclude that in 1 Cor. 7:15 the phrase 'in such cases' should be understood to include *any cases that similarly destroy a marriage*," and abuse is such a case. His position is scholarly, and many counselors and pastors agree. A LifeWay Research survey found that 55 percent of pastors believe divorce may be the best option in cases of domestic violence. The Evangelical Theological Society audience who read Grudem's paper and heard him speak was "overwhelmingly positive and appreciative."[10] I always counsel couples to do everything possible to resolve their strains and mend a broken relationship, but it takes two to make it work, and as Paul explained, that's not always possible.

THE ROLE OF PRAYER

When dealing with difficult people, one of the most important things you can do is pray. Prayer invites God into the situation and allows Him to work in both your heart and the heart of the other person. James 1:5 (NIV) encourages us to ask God for wisdom: "If any of you lacks wisdom, you should ask God, who gives generously to all without finding fault, and it will be given to you." Whether you're unsure of how to handle a difficult person or struggling to maintain a positive attitude, prayer is a powerful tool that can guide you in your interactions.

Dealing with difficult people is an inevitable part of life, but how you choose to respond makes all the difference.

When we read the Gospels, we see Jesus dealing with difficult people on nearly every page. We immediately think of the

Pharisees and Sadducees, who hated and opposed Him at every turn. How did Jesus treat them? He spent time with Nicodemus to explain what it means to be born again. He went to dinner at Simon's house, and He must have interacted with Joseph of Arimathea at some point. But in Matthew 23, Jesus also "spoke truth to power" in the seven "woes," rebuking them for their hard hearts. Jesus was incredibly patient with the disciples, who consistently misunderstood Him and argued about who would be the top dog when Jesus inaugurated His kingdom. Tax collectors weren't like IRS agents today; they were Jews who collaborated with the Roman occupiers. The rest of the Jewish people despised them, but Jesus went to Zacchaeus' house. He ate with tax collectors and prostitutes, and in that day, eating with someone demonstrated acceptance. The Bible tells us He was "a friend of sinners." Jesus reached out to touch lepers, the lame, the blind, and even the dead, bringing healing and life when others assumed their condition was a product of sin that disqualified them from the family of God.

But that's not the end of the story. Paul reminds us that we were also enemies of God—sinful outcasts beyond hope—until Jesus died the death we deserved so we could share the blessed life He deserved to live. When we were difficult people, Jesus poured out His love, forgiveness, and acceptance.

> Jesus told the people listening on the mountain: "For if you love those who love you, what reward have you? Do not even the tax collectors do the same? And if you greet your brethren only, what do you do more than others? Do not even the tax collectors do so? Therefore you shall be perfect, just as your Father in heaven is perfect."
>
> —MATTHEW 5:46–48

When we consider that Jesus loved us when we were unlovable, our attitudes change toward those who are hard to love.

Consider this:

1. Review the kinds of difficult people in this chapter. Which ones have created the biggest headaches for you? (No names, please!)

2. Do you see yourself in any of the descriptions? If you do, which one(s)? How do you feel about this self-awareness?

3. How does it (or might it) help to understand what may have caused a person to be difficult?

4. Review the principles of responding instead of reacting. Which of these do you do well? Which do you need to work on? What difference will it make?

5. Some of us instinctively set clear boundaries and enforce them, but most of us don't. What truths in this section do you need to internalize? What boundaries do you need to establish and enforce? Write a plan to make it happen.

6. Look at the Matthew 5 passage again. Who are individuals or classes of people who are hard to love? In this passage's context, what does it mean to be "perfect"?

> "WHEN CONFLICTS ARISE, OUR ATTITUDE CAN EITHER ADD FUEL TO THE FIRE OR BRING PEACE AND HEALING."

Chapter 5

THE DEATH OF A DREAM

Hope deferred makes the heart sick,
but when the desire comes, it is a tree of life.
—Proverbs 13:12

I think I was born with a baseball in one hand and a football in the other. From the day I could walk and saw older kids playing sports, I wanted to go onto the field and join them. My first love was baseball. Even as a little boy, I could throw hard and had good control, so my coach put me in as the pitcher. When I was twelve, the newspaper featured an article about me and called me "a prodigy." The reporter described the boys I struck out as walking back to the dugout in a daze. You would have thought I was the second coming of Sandy Koufax!

In high school I excelled, and like tens of thousands of other boys that age, I dreamed of being drafted and playing in the major leagues. My driving motivation was to make enough money to buy my mother a nice house. But throwing curveballs is sometimes destructive to a young arm, and I did permanent damage to my arm. When the doctor told me I was finished, I was devastated. All my daydreams, all the accolades, and all my confidence evaporated in a single moment.

Years later, when I had the thrill of leading my mother to Christ, I realized my dream was being fulfilled far better than I'd ever imagined. I had dreamed of building her an earthly home, but God built her a heavenly one, and He used me to begin to show it to her. When she was in her last days in the hospital, she asked everyone to leave the room, but she motioned for me to stay. She whispered, "Son, I want you to preach my funeral. Will you do that for me?"

I took a deep breath and explained, "Mom, you're asking something really hard from me."

She smiled and said, "But nobody can talk about me like you."

I couldn't say no to her. "OK, I'll do it."

When Mom died, I asked the Lord what He wanted me to say about her at the funeral, and I told the story of my baseball career and my vision of building Mom a home. When I explained that the death of my baseball dream had ultimately led to the fulfillment of the bigger dream to help prepare my mother for the home in heaven with Jesus, there were a lot of tears in the audience, including mine.

THE CYCLE

Unless we're suffering from clinical depression, most of us are motivated by a vision of a better life. Our dreams can focus on almost any endeavor: getting married, having a child, graduating, securing a good job, getting a promotion, launching a business, winning the lottery, taking a wonderful vacation, finding a cure for cancer, or making a difference in some other way that changes lives.

We can identify four stages in the cycle of a dream:

1. Birth

When the vision begins to congeal in our minds and hearts, it's thrilling. We imagine the possibilities, and we're excited. We strategize, create plans, and share our dreams with anyone who will listen.

2. Growth

The first steps are challenging but promising. The idea begins to take shape, and we realize it will take more of us than we thought. But we also receive encouragement from those who are watching us take bold steps, so we're eager to keep going.

3. Death

We may see it coming, or it may come out of the blue. We hit roadblocks we didn't anticipate—we realize we didn't have enough resources, the economy changes, or someone we trusted let us down. Instead of marrying the person of our dreams, he or she changes direction, leaving us feeling empty, lonely, and devastated. We were thrilled when the pregnancy test was positive, but then came the miscarriage or the terrible diagnosis from the doctor about our baby. Instead of a promotion, the CEO sent a letter saying he was downsizing and eliminating our position. On our dream vacation, we got the flu, our wallet was stolen, or we got caught in an international incident. Or like me, we had high hopes that we could do something special for someone we love, but it didn't work out. The dream may have died a slow death, or it could have been sudden, but the cold, hard truth is that it's deceased.

4. Rebirth

When a dream dies, we go through a process that's similar to grieving the death of someone we love. The stages aren't linear. We often take one step forward and two steps back, but if we stay with it, we regain a fresh sense of hope. At first, we can't believe it's happened; we're in denial. We rationalize that if God was in it, it couldn't fail. The next stage is anger, which is often coupled with self-pity. We point to those who let us down (including God) and pour out our resentment. We then may have flashes of false hope: "If I just did this differently, if only that happened, if I could get them to help, I could save this thing!" This is clinging to what some have called a "hopeless hope." When the full weight of the loss and the hopelessness of rescue hits, we feel crushed. We don't see any way forward, and we face the fact that our hopes have been dashed. We feel the loss, we grieve, and over time hope is rekindled—but it's a different hope.

From the corpse of our dream, something begins to stir. God gives us a new idea, one that is different from before but somehow better. For me, the dream of pitching for a major-league club was replaced with the dream of seeing God use me to help change lives. Before, I had focused on changing one life by building my mom a home, but God has given me the unspeakable privilege of touching the lives of countless people—including my mom.

"But Why?"

It's a question I asked a million times when I hurt my arm, and others ask the same question every time a dream bites the dust. We can't read God's mind to know the exact reason each time, but we can be sure our pain isn't because He doesn't love us. The cross is the flashing neon sign that reminds us that everything God does is for our good and His glory. We need to start there, but He might have more pointed reasons—for instance:

- **To refine us**

Malachi, the last of the Old Testament prophets, predicted the "messenger" would come before God made His appearance. He didn't understand it then, but we have the benefit of hindsight: Hundreds of years later God sent John the Baptist to play the role of Elijah and announce the coming King. But Malachi warns that God's people weren't ready. They needed to go through a process of being refined, cleansed, and purified. He wrote:

> But who can endure the day of His coming? And who can stand when He appears? For He is like a refiner's fire and like launderers' soap. He will sit as a refiner and a purifier of silver; He will purify the sons of Levi, and purge them as gold and silver, that they may offer to the LORD an offering in righteousness.
>
> —MALACHI 3:2–3

Who among us is so out of touch with our hearts that we don't think we need to be refined? Paul spends large sections of his letters teaching his first readers, and us, that God's grace saves us, but our attitudes and behaviors often still stink. He gives clear directives to change course but not just on the outside. He wants our motives to be purified by a richer, deeper grasp of the wonder of God's love. Confession and repentance put us in the refiner's fire and the washbasin. When gold and silver are purified, they're heated so the impurities are burned away, leaving the pure metal. When dirty clothes go into the wash, they don't just sit there. They're agitated so the detergent can dissolve every speck of dirt.

The death of a dream is a refiner's fire and a washbasin. Does God care about His people being purified? Would you be happy with a piece of gold jewelry that looks like a dusty rock? Would you want to wear filthy clothes? Of course He cares, but our adoption into His family isn't based on the level of our purity; otherwise, none of us would make it! He accepts us into His family in whatever dusty, filthy, unpurified condition in which we come to Him. In Paul's brilliant letter to the Christians in Rome, he spends chapters defining and describing salvation by grace through faith. In chapter 5, he begins by recounting what he'd written in the first four chapters:

> Therefore, having been justified by faith, we have peace with God through our Lord Jesus Christ, through whom also we have access by faith into this grace in which we stand, and rejoice in hope of the glory of God.
> —Romans 5:1–2

Then Paul explains that the glory of God isn't only revealed through Jesus dying to save us; we see His glory when His people trust Him when life seems upside down:

> And not only that, but we also glory in tribulations, knowing that tribulation produces perseverance; and perseverance, character; and character, hope. Now hope does not disappoint, because the love of God has been poured out in our hearts by the Holy Spirit who was given to us.
> —Romans 5:3–5

The progression is important: When our attitudes are filled with faith, we're resilient and persevering in the face of difficulties. Holding tight to God when we can't see what He's doing builds our character, and over time a God-honoring character produces the commodity we can't live without, in good times and bad: hope. When we stare at the death of our dream, we despair, but when our hope is fixed on God's sovereignty and goodness, the Holy Spirit makes God's love more real to us than ever. Isn't that what you want? Sure, it is.

Refining isn't fun, but it's necessary. While God accepts us in whatever filthy condition we come to Him, He loves us too much to let us stay there. Those of us who have walked with God a long time aren't surprised when He takes us through another furnace of fire. The first time was a shock to our systems, but no longer. We don't enjoy it, and we don't like it, but we know God is doing something wonderful *in us*, and someday, as we learn the lessons, *through us*.

- **To redirect us**

God may allow the death of a dream to alter our course. We may have been drifting (or sprinting) toward something that would detour us away from God's best, or He may have something better for us, and He knows we'll stay where we are until we have to move. I wish I always responded to the gentle nudge of the Spirit, but sometimes I need a shove!

Paul was an incredible leader. He was one of the most influential people the world has ever known: bold, resourceful, and tenacious in following God's will. That's why I'm fascinated by an often overlooked passage in Luke's account of the early church. Paul had recently attended the Jerusalem Council to debate what it would take for gentiles to be admitted into the church. It was one of the most significant meetings in church history. Some had insisted that the gentiles become Jews (through circumcision and following the dietary laws) before they could become Christians, but Peter and Paul explained how God had given the Spirit to gentiles without those requirements. I have no idea how things might have turned out if the decision had gone with the legalists, but Paul left on his next mission with the good news that gentiles were fully accepted into the family of God by faith alone.

Paul traveled back to the region that is now central Turkey to visit the churches he'd planted on his first trip and give them the good news from the council. Then, he planned to go west to an area he'd never been to before. Luke tells us, "Now when they had gone through Phrygia and the region of Galatia, they were forbidden by the Holy Spirit to preach the word in Asia. After they had come to Mysia, they tried to go into Bithynia, but the Spirit did not permit them" (Acts 16:6–7).

Can you see it? Paul set out for the area called Asia, but the Holy Spirit said, "No, not this way." Then he planned to go to Bithynia, but the Spirit again said, "Uh-uh, Paul. Not there either." Was God finished with Paul? Were these nos the end for him? Not in the least. Luke continues, "So passing by Mysia, they came down to Troas. And a vision appeared to Paul in the night. A man of Macedonia stood and pleaded with him, saying, 'Come over to Macedonia and help us.' Now after he had seen the vision, immediately we sought to go to Macedonia, concluding that the Lord had called us to preach the gospel to them" (Acts 16:8–10). God was redirecting Paul to launch the church in Europe! God opened doors in Philippi, Thessalonica, Berea, Athens, and Corinth, and the gospel spread to both Jews and gentiles.

God uses many ways to communicate which way He wants us to go, and one of those is sometimes a big *no* to our previous plans. When a door closes, we can have a sour attitude and complain for a long time, or we can, with the eyes of faith,

The Death of a Dream

look for the open door where God wants us to go. A roadblock need not be the end of the road; instead, it can be a detour to something better.

Joe had a job he loved, and he poured his heart into it. He took a job at another company—a promotion with higher pay. He was sure that was exactly where God wanted him to be. He excelled there too—until the company went bankrupt. He applied to other companies, but the economy was tanking around the country, especially in his industry. Instead of finding a great new job, he had to scramble just to make some money to provide for his family. It was a really tough time for Joe. After six months of emotional turmoil, someone he barely knew called and asked if he wanted a short-term consulting job in a different industry. It didn't seem to fit, but Joe was desperate. He did well in that role, and soon others called to ask him to serve in the same capacity at their companies. Joe felt an odd blend of gratitude, discouragement, and confusion. He was glad to make some money, but he missed his previous role, and he couldn't understand why God still hadn't opened doors in his chosen field. Two years later (he admits he's a slow learner), God gave him the revelation that consulting with multiple companies was exactly where He wanted him. This way he was able to share his expertise—and his heart for Christ—with many different leaders all over the country.

- **For God's glory**

When your best friend calls you at two o'clock in the morning, what do you do? You get up, throw on some clothes, and go to them. Mary and Martha rang Jesus' phone to tell Him their brother, Lazarus, was very sick, but Jesus didn't rush to his side. The disciples were perplexed. They knew Jesus loved those three, and they'd seen Him heal all kinds of illnesses and conditions, but He told them, "This sickness is not unto death, but for the glory of God, that the Son of God may be glorified through it" (John 11:4).

If I'd been one of the disciples, I would have thought, "Great. Healings glorify God. OK, let's go!" But Jesus stayed two more days. Finally, He announced that they were going to Lazarus' home and the sisters in Bethany, which was in Judea—the very region where a mob had threatened to stone Jesus earlier. The disciples questioned His sanity: "Rabbi, lately the Jews sought to stone You, and are You going there again?" (John 11:8). They were even more confused when Jesus told them Lazarus was asleep, but He would wake him up. Why in the world would they need to travel several days to wake up someone who was sleeping? Jesus told them bluntly that Lazarus was dead, and then He explained, "And I am glad for your sakes that I was not there, that you may believe. Nevertheless, let us go to him" (John 11:15). Always the optimist, Thomas may have uttered under his breath (or maybe it was a stage whisper so everyone could hear): "Let us also go, that we may die with Him" (John 11:16).

After several days they arrived in Bethany. The sisters had buried their brother four days earlier. Imagine being one of the sisters. This was the death of their dear brother, but it was also the death of their expectations of their friend Jesus. They had sent for Him, but He didn't come in time. Their disappointment in Jesus compounded their grief over their brother's death.

When they heard Jesus was approaching, each of the sisters went out to talk to Him. It appears they'd shared their disappointment with each other, because both said, "Lord, if You had been here, my brother would not have died" (John 11:21, 32). In other words, "It's Your fault! You could have healed him, but now he's dead."

Jesus wasn't an emotionless stoic. His decision to wait had hurt those He loved, but it was for a greater purpose. When He saw those who were weeping, "He groaned in the spirit and was troubled" (John 11:33). This means He was heartbroken, shaken to the core, and He wept with them. When they escorted Jesus to the tomb, some ridiculed Him. Jesus told some people to roll the stone away from the tomb's entrance. Martha protested that the stench would be overpowering, but Jesus assured her, "Did I not say to you that if you would believe you would see the glory of God?" (John 11:40). Jesus called Lazarus to come out, and the dead man came to life.

What was the response of those watching that day? Some believed in Jesus, but others ratted on Him, telling the Pharisees who plotted from that day on to kill Him. John recorded this event and those painful conversations to show that the diamond of God's glory often sparkles most brilliantly against the backdrop of dark suffering. When you and I suffer the death of our dreams, we almost certainly feel betrayed like Mary and Martha when Jesus showed up late. But if we follow Him to the tomb of our hopes, God can do something so dramatic that we stand in wonder.

When I hurt my throwing arm and my dream of a career in baseball died, God used it in three ways: I went into the refiner's fire to purify my motives, God redirected me to the ministry, and I saw the greater glory of my mother and father trusting in Jesus. Was it worth it? Oh, yeah.

Unexpected

Seldom has a dream died more painfully than when Jerusalem was overrun and destroyed by the Babylonians. God's people never imagined Solomon's temple would be torn down. They were sure God wouldn't let that happen, but it did. Daniel and his three friends, along with others from the upper part of society, were taken into exile to serve the conquering king. As a Jewish community in Babylon, they longed for home.

The prophet Hananiah told them what they wanted to hear: The exile would last only two years. They'd return home with all the holy vessels taken from the temple, and a new Jewish king would be crowned. But Hananiah was just playing on their hurts—God hadn't promised that at all. The prophet Jeremiah confronted him and pronounced a sentence of death.

Jeremiah had a very different message for the exiles, one they didn't expect. Instead of counting the days for two years until they would leave, he told them they'd be exiles for seventy years. And even more astounding was that God wanted them to have a *positive* attitude, even in exile. Instead of despising the Babylonians, God wanted them to be the light of God's love and the salt that flavored their interactions. His instructions were specific:

> Build houses and dwell in them; plant gardens and eat their fruit. Take wives and beget sons and daughters; and take wives for your sons and give your daughters to husbands, so that they may bear sons and daughters—that you may be increased there, and not diminished. And seek the peace of the city where I have caused you to be carried away captive, and pray to the LORD for it; for in its peace you will have peace.
>
> —JEREMIAH 29:5–7

Instead of cursing, bless. Instead of complaining, give thanks. Instead of tearing down, build up. Instead of casting resentment, pray for the peace of Babylon. Was God being cruel by asking them to bless those who had captured them? No. A few verses later He explained:

> For I know the thoughts that I think toward you, says the Lord, thoughts of peace and not of evil, to give you a future and a hope. Then you will call upon Me and go and pray to Me, and I will listen to you. And you will seek Me and find Me, when you search for Me with all your heart. I will be found by you, says the Lord, and I will bring you back from your captivity; I will gather you from all the nations and from all the places where I have driven you, says the Lord, and I will bring you to the place from which I cause you to be carried away captive.
> —Jeremiah 29:11–14

God's agenda is *usually* different from ours, and it's *always* bigger and better. If we insist we can't trust Him if He doesn't let us in on His secret plans, we'll live stunted, confused, and resentful lives.

When David walked out on that field to meet Goliath, he had no armor or military training—just a slingshot, five stones, and unshakable faith in God. He was just a kid; Goliath was, well, a Goliath! David had every reason to turn the other way and run! No one expected David to win, but he wasn't relying on himself. He trusted God to give him courage, strength, and accurate aim. His story reminds us that we don't need every tool in the toolbox to be successful, but we certainly need faith in the God of the impossible.

Thomas Edison was resilient in the face of failure. Before he discovered the right filament for light bulbs, he tried thousands that didn't work. His lab was filled with broken experiments and discarded ideas, but he never gave up. He saw failure as part of the process. He is famously quoted as having said, "I haven't failed. I've just found 10,000 ways that won't work."

We can learn from David and Edison. When we're faced with unimaginable challenges, rejection, and failure, it doesn't mean we should give up or that we're finished. God might be leading us to something bigger and better than we ever imagined. The key is to keep going, to trust that every setback and detour is part of the journey, and to believe that even in our deepest disappointments God is working to create something wonderful—both in us and through us.

Missing the Point

In Palestine in the first century, the Jewish people had been under the heel of the Greeks and then the Romans. They had a brief period of independence when Judas Maccabeus defeated the Greeks under Antiochus Epiphanes, who erected a statue of Zeus in Solomon's temple and sacrificed a pig on the Lord's altar. But only a few years later the Romans captured the land. When Jesus came along, the Jews expected the Messiah to do three things: cleanse the temple, expel the Romans from the land, and establish David's throne again. As the disciples followed Jesus and saw His miracles, they believed that He was "the guy." He cleansed the temple. One down! When He arrived in Jerusalem after raising Lazarus, He rode a donkey as people shouted, "Hosanna to the King!" His triumphal entry was like (but also not like) Roman generals who rode fine horses into Rome, leading their armies and captured slaves. The disciples probably thought, "Well, it's not quite what I expected, but we've got a week before Passover."

The Death of a Dream

They were convinced that Passover—that weekend—would be the turning point in the history of God's people. They were absolutely right—and tragically wrong. Jesus is the King, but His kingdom is upside down from what the disciples (and many others) expected. The last shall be first, and the first last; to be great, be a servant of all; to have real life, you have to die to yourself. That's not what the disciples signed up for! They believed Jesus would conquer the Romans and be crowned king. And them? They'd be His cabinet running departments of the kingdom.

At the Passover meal, when Jesus explained the broken bread represented His broken body and the wine represented His blood that would be shed to establish the new covenant, the disciples argued about which of them would be the greatest on Jesus' staff! I can imagine Jesus shaking His head as He explained (again):

> "The kings of the Gentiles exercise lordship over them, and those who exercise authority over them are called 'benefactors.' But not so among you; on the contrary, he who is greatest among you, let him be as the younger, and he who governs as he who serves. For who is greater, he who sits at the table, or he who serves? Is it not he who sits at the table? Yet I am among you as the One who serves.
> —Luke 22:25–27

That night, Jesus was arrested, tried in a kangaroo court, and mocked. The next day, He was tortured and executed. This was the literal death of the disciples' dream! But three days later Jesus came out of the tomb and appeared to them for the next forty days.

The disciples missed the point over and over again. It wasn't until the Holy Spirit descended on them at Pentecost that they understood that God's dream was quite different from theirs.

Each of us, if our hearts are beating, has dreams, but those dreams sometimes wither away and sometimes are crushed in an instant. If we dig deep and develop an attitude of hope, we'll see God refining us, redirecting us to something better, and glorifying Himself as we trust Him.

Consider this:

1. Among the people you know, what dreams have you seen die? How did people initially react? How did they respond in the long run?

2. How about you? Describe a time when your dream died. What lessons did God teach you in that experience?

3. What does God's refining fire look like and feel like? What are the challenges of believing God when we're in the fire?

4. How does God redirect people? What are some ways He gets our attention and guides us?

5. Is the concept of God's "greater glory" hard to grasp? Why or why not? What experiences in your life have been hard but brought God glory?

6. Look again at the two passages from Jeremiah 29 in this chapter. What are parallels today of God instructing us to bless those who have a very different agenda from ours, and God's promise of "a future and a hope" if we trust in Him?

7. Why is it important to expect (or at least be open to) the unexpected that God brings our way?

> "WHEN WE STARE AT THE DEATH OF OUR DREAM, WE DESPAIR, BUT WHEN OUR HOPE IS FIXED ON GOD'S SOVEREIGNTY AND GOODNESS, THE HOLY SPIRIT MAKES GOD'S LOVE MORE REAL TO US THAN EVER."

Chapter 6

THE POWER OF WORDS

*Death and life are in the power of the tongue,
and those who love it will eat its fruit.*
—Proverbs 18:21

When I was a boy, my mother's positive attitude and her belief in me gave me confidence in myself; she spoke life into me every chance she got. Some people who watched me told my mother I was "conceited," but she told them, "No, Theodore is just convinced!" My positive self-image was entirely the product of my mother's influence and example. I lived every day hearing my father's derogatory words toward her. I have many memories of him walking in the door after work and instantly berating her, calling her names, and accusing her of sins he was committing. I often tried to step in to defend her, but he waved me off, insisting, "You don't understand. You don't know what's going on!"

I was affected by his abuse of my mother as if it were secondhand smoke. His messages would have ruined me if my mother's kindness and consistency hadn't overcome the poison of his words.

What we say matters more than we often realize. Our words can either lift someone up or tear them down. They can fuel hope or feed fear. Jesus understood this better than anyone. He didn't merely speak to be heard—His words brought healing, redemption, and life. Whether comforting the broken, challenging the self-righteous, or teaching through parables, every word He spoke carried purpose. His voice calmed storms—both literal and spiritual—proving that words infused with faith and love have power beyond measure.

Words and Attitude

We can't separate our attitudes from the words we speak. In the famous passage in James' letter to the church, he explains that we have the power and responsibility to choose our words, which then shape our attitudes. Our words are like a bridle controlling a powerful horse or a rudder steering a ship. But our attitudes also affect the words that come out of our mouths. James seems to be exasperated that his readers have such little control over their tongues. He chastens them (and us):

> But no man can tame the tongue. It is an unruly evil, full of deadly poison. With it we bless our God and Father, and with it we curse men, who have been made in the similitude of God. Out of the same mouth proceed blessing and cursing. My brethren, these things ought not to be so. Does a spring send forth fresh water and bitter from the same opening? Can a fig tree, my brethren, bear olives, or a grapevine bear figs? Thus no spring yields both salt water and fresh.
> —James 3:8–12

In the Scriptures we see the profound impact of our words:

1. What we think shapes what we say.

Solomon explained:

> Keep your heart with all diligence, for out of it spring the issues of life. Put away from you a deceitful mouth, and put perverse lips far from you.
> —PROVERBS 4:23–24

Similarly, Jesus explained: "A good man out of the good treasure of his heart brings forth good; and an evil man out of the evil treasure of his heart brings forth evil. For out of the abundance of the heart his mouth speaks" (Luke 6:45).

2. Our words can breathe life or cause death.

You know how it feels when someone sees something good in you and calls it out, and you know the devastation caused by words spoken in contempt. As actress Celeste Holm observed, "We live by encouragement and die without it—slowly, sadly, and angrily." An anonymous but wise person commented, "Don't mix bad words with your bad mood. You'll have many opportunities to change a mood, but you'll never get the opportunity to replace the words you spoke." And Mother Teresa remarked, "Kind words can be short and easy to speak, but their echoes are truly endless."[11]

We can also speak life or death to ourselves. When I play golf and hit a bad shot, I tell myself, "Come on, Ted! You've got this. Make the next shot a good one." (Tonia sometimes wonders if talking to myself is a sign that I'm losing my mind, but I explain that this is actually how I *keep* my sanity.)

3. Our words have the power to heal or hurt.

Words can hurt in many different ways. They can crush a person's heart, create self-doubt, rob them of confidence, instill fear and shame, instantly shatter or gradually erode trust, inflame anxiety, and create isolation.

People are wounded in relationships and healed in relationships. Positive words can salve the hurts of the past and present, create bonds of trust and affection, inspire people to take steps forward, reduce anxiety, and instill confidence about the future.

Solomon noted:

> Pleasant words are like a honeycomb, sweetness to the soul and health to the bones.
> —PROVERBS 16:24

I often remind people in our church that the enemy wants to use our words to "steal, kill, and destroy," but God can infuse our words with enough grace, kindness, and power to change the course of someone's life.

4. We have responsibility over our words.

As we saw earlier, Paul commanded us to "speak the truth in love," which always involves a choice. In Ephesians 4 he describes several choices: Don't lie, but speak the truth. Be angry, but don't sin in your anger. Stop stealing, but work hard so you can be generous. Get rid of bitterness, but be kind and forgiving. There's one more on his short list: "Let no corrupt word proceed out of your mouth, but what is good for necessary edification, that it may impart grace to the hearers" (Ephesians 4:29).

Each of the positives and negatives in this section of the letter shows us a clear choice. If we choose harmful, cutting, or contemptuous words that put others down so we feel power over them, it hurts God's heart. Paul puts it this way: "And do not grieve the Holy Spirit of God, by whom you were sealed for the day of redemption" (Ephesians 4:30). When our words harm people, God is sad. Words like those aren't consistent with who we are today as chosen, adopted, forgiven, and sealed children of the King, and they're not consistent with who we will one day be when God makes all things new. When we are obedient to use our words to bless, build, and encourage, we partner with God to bring glimpses of the glory of the future into the present.

5. Affirming others has a positive impact on us.

Messages are naturally reciprocal. When we're harsh to others, our hearts harden a bit more, but when we encourage someone and see the light of love and joy in their faces, we experience great satisfaction. Think of the joy of smiling at a baby and the baby smiling back. And think of the deep satisfaction of speaking words of encouragement to a son or daughter who is taking big steps, such as starting a career or getting married. We see the impact of our affirmation, and we have the thrill of knowing we've made a positive difference.

Three Kinds of People

On a broad continuum we can identify three kinds of people: those who are habitually caustic and tear people down, those who give mixed messages, and those who regularly use their words to build people up. I have some advice for each one.

- **Caustic people**

I've known people who are either so arrogant that they don't care about others or are so insecure that their way to cope is to always be in a position of power. Either way, they use condemnation, accusation, sarcasm, isolation, and other means to put people down. They need to realize their hurtful messages hurt everyone who hears them, even themselves. Damaging words have no winners; affirming words have no losers.

Passive-aggressive behavior is a favorite tactic of those who seek power and control over others while appearing innocent. They can cut someone to shreds, and when the person looks hurt, they claim, "Hey, I was only kidding!" As if that makes the pain go away. Or they "push the buttons" of someone close to them without appearing to be selfish or destructive. If they know their spouse or friend values being on time, they find reasons to be late. When they see the other person get frustrated, they make excuses: "I couldn't help it. I had to feed the dog." Passive-aggressive words are designed to stab with a sharp knife, but the excuse is an attempt to wipe the blood off and appear innocent.

If your spouse or best friend has the courage to tell you that your words are full of poison, don't write them off. Listen, ask for examples, and don't bully them into backing down. If you keep up the power move to dominate people, you'll ruin your most important relationships and quite possibly have stress-related health problems.

- **Mixed messages**

A friend told me that his mother's communication with him kept him off balance: "One day she would be loving, affirming, and encouraging, but the next day she was critical, and nothing would satisfy her."

I asked, "How did that affect you? Could you block out the negative and focus on the positive?"

He laughed, but it was a nervous laugh. "I wish! I'm afraid I absorbed the negative and distrusted the positive. I wish it had been the other way around."

Psychologists say mixed messages are more manipulative than consistently positive or negative ones. When a person's messages are fairly uniform, the recipients know where they stand, but mixed messages create confusion and insecurity.

A second form of mixed messages happens in the moment: A person can say, "I love you," but with such a sour disposition or passivity that the nonverbal communication drowns out the words. The hearer wants to believe the words, but the facial expression or tone of voice screams something entirely different.

If someone loves you enough to call out your mixed messages, don't make excuses or shut down the conversation. Listen, listen some more, and invite the person to point out, in the moment, when you're giving mixed messages. Pay attention to the other person's response to see if your communication accomplishes what you intend.

- **Consistently positive**

Way to go! Keep it up! If God has melted and molded your heart so you're filled and overflowing with His love, your words have a powerful impact on those around you. You're a great blessing to others, and God smiles on you. Of course, you're human and you still make mistakes; in those moments simply recognize when you've communicated something other than "grace and truth," and make it right.

Through the good times and difficulties of your life, continue to find God faithful and loving. More often than not, rest in Him and enjoy His presence. My advice to you is, "Excel still more!" Ask God to give you continued discernment so you can speak the right words—those may sometimes be corrective, but still, remain affirming. Solomon put the two together:

> A word fitly spoken is like apples of gold in settings of silver. Like an earring of gold and an ornament of fine gold is a wise rebuker to an obedient ear.
> —PROVERBS 25:11–12

EXPOSED

One of the chief marks of spiritual maturity is sensitivity to the Spirit's whisper that something we've said or done grieves Him. Some churches don't talk much about confession and repentance these days because awareness of sin makes a lot of people feel uncomfortable. News flash: It should! There are, though, two kinds of repentance. One type is full of condemnation and shame. In this case the misguided solution is to feel bad enough long enough, but it's never over before the next moment of condemnation and shame, thus rendering it perpetual. The other kind of repentance accepts the truth that we've sinned, but it reminds us that Jesus has completely paid the price for our sins. His last words on the cross were, "It is finished." It wasn't just that His life was over; it was that the debt for sin had been paid for all time. In this case repentance reconnects us to the source of our security and significance—the life, death, and resurrection of Jesus. Instead of shame, we feel relieved and refreshed.

David's beautiful prayer in Psalm 139 is about the omniscience, omnipotence, and omnipresence of God. He affirms that God has created him with specific gifts, talents, and opportunities:

> I will praise You, for I am fearfully and wonderfully made; marvelous are Your works, and that my soul knows very well.
> —PSALM 139:14

At the end of the psalm, David feels known and loved, so he has no fear in asking God to expose anything and everything in him that displeases God:

> Search me, O God, and know my heart; try me, and know my anxieties; and see if there is any wicked way in me, and lead me in the way everlasting.
> —Psalm 139:23–24

The way we use our words may be the most obvious expression of what's in our hearts. If we ask God to search us, know us, and try our words, we'll probably realize that some of them have missed the high standards of "no unwholesome word" and "only those that encourage those who hear." The appropriate response is to agree with God that we've sinned, agree with Him that Christ's sacrifice paid for that sin, and agree with Him that His best is for us to use our words carefully and graciously.

When He searches us, the Spirit may also expose wounds caused by someone else's words. We then must reflect deeply on God's forgiveness of us as the source of power to forgive those who sin against us. Continuing in the passage in Ephesians, Paul clarified things for us: "Let all bitterness, wrath, anger, clamor, and evil speaking be put away from you, with all malice. And be kind to one another, tenderhearted, forgiving one another, even as God in Christ forgave you" (Ephesians 4:31–32).

Forgiveness is a hard but necessary work. It's far easier to remain stuck in resentment and self-pity, hiding behind the convenient excuse "I'm the one who was wronged!" Precisely. No one is arguing that you weren't wronged, but God has provided a way to be free of the bitterness. Author and Pastor

Lewis Smedes advises us to be totally honest about what happened—no minimizing or excusing the person:

> When we forgive evil we do not excuse it, we do not tolerate it, we do not smother it. We look the evil full in the face, call it what it is, let its horror shock and stun and enrage us, and only then do we forgive it.[12]

When Jesus forgave us, He absorbed the debt. In the same way, when we forgive those who have hurt us, we absorb their debt. In *The Reason for God*, Pastor Tim Keller explains:

> Forgiveness means refusing to make them pay for what they did. However, to refrain from lashing out at someone when you want to do so with all your being is *agony*. It is a form of suffering. You not only suffer the original loss of happiness, reputation, and opportunity, but now you forgo the consolation of inflicting the same on them. You are absorbing the debt, taking the cost of it completely on yourself instead of taking it out of the other person. It hurts terribly. Many people would say it feels like a kind of death. Yes, but it is a death that leads to resurrection instead of the lifelong living death of bitterness and cynicism.[13]

It's very helpful to explore the root causes of shame, which is the exposure of our flaws but without the healing and cleansing of forgiveness, and it's instructive to look under our sinful words to see if our harsh, condemning language comes from deep insecurity or simply the sin of wanting to dominate others. Listen to the Lord. He'll show you.

EXAMPLES

Throughout the letters of the New Testament we find "one another" passages. We aren't meant to be Lone Rangers—the westernized model of the "rugged individualist" isn't found in Scripture. We're part of a body, and if one person suffers, all of us are affected. God has given me some wonderful people who have spoken into my life and modeled a lifestyle of fervent optimism, including my mother; my sister Val; Tonia; and my mentor, L. H. Hardwick, who was the pastor at Christ's Church in Nashville for fifty-five years. He always treated me with grace and dignity, whether I lived up to expectations or not. I think he and my mother were cut from the same cloth—both were consistently kind and encouraging, and the love of Jesus spilled out of them in every interaction. When I was off track, he corrected me, often by saying something like, "Ted, here's why we're not going to do it that way again," but he always ended the conversation with words of affirmation.

When we planted Center Point Church, I asked Pastor Hardwick to come and speak a few times. During the week he taught leadership principles to my staff, and then he preached on Sunday morning. Each time he came, he made a point of meeting personally with me to speak words of life and hope, affirming God's call on my life and encouraging us in our church's progress. I remember him looking into my eyes and saying, "This is just the beginning of all God wants to do in you and through you, Ted. You've come a long way, but the half has not yet been told."

In all the years I knew him and spent one-on-one time with him, I don't recall ever hearing a negative word come out of his mouth. He was realistic; he didn't sugarcoat problems, but he saw opportunities in the face of obstacles and a hopeful future in those who had failed.

When I played football in high school, we had a coaching change between my junior and senior years. The new guy,

Coach Crass, called each of the players into his office to get to know them. When I sat down in front of his desk, he said, "Ted, I understand you're a phenomenal athlete, but I want to know if you know where you'll spend eternity when you die."

Surprised, I stammered, "Well, I guess I'll go to heaven."

Coach sat back and smiled. "You guess?"

"Yeah," I said, looking for a good answer. "I'm a pretty good person. I don't hurt anybody."

He answered, "Your goodness isn't going to get you there." He paused for a few seconds and then said, "We'll talk about this later."

A week or two later Coach invited me to attend a meeting of the Fellowship of Christian Athletes (FCA). It was the event I described in the first chapter. That night was when I truly understood the gospel of grace. I trusted Christ, and my life was changed forever.

Coach caught a lot of grief from parents for taking a stand for Christ. Some mocked him for praying with the team. I remember one dad sneering, "Does he think he's going to pray his way to a win?" He was a good coach but an even better follower of Jesus. He was bold in sharing his faith, and my relationship with Christ resulted from his love for his players.

Years later, after I started in ministry, Coach Crass asked me to speak to his students. Before I got up, he introduced me: "Ted doesn't know it yet, but I'll tell you a story about him. When he was on our team, he gave his life to Christ at a revival. Ted was a popular student, and God used him to spread the good news. A year after he became a Christian, the FCA regional director gave me stats about our local chapter. Through Ted's direct influence 163 students trusted in Jesus."

The Power of Words

Coach Crass sat down, and I stood up, but I could hardly talk because I was weeping with joy and amazement that God could use someone like me.

Our words matter. They have enormous power to touch hearts and change lives. Use them well.

Consider this:

1. Describe how your words affect your attitude. Now describe how your attitude affects your words.

2. Who has spoken life-giving words over you? What were the circumstances? What impact did that have on you, your thoughts, perceptions, or actions?

3. Have you been the victim of caustic words? If so, how long did it last, and how were you affected?

4. Why do you think mixed messages are so confusing?

5. Describe the two kinds of repentance. What's the damage done by shame? What's the blessing of reconnecting with the grace of God?

6. Take some time to reflect on Psalm 139:23–24. What is God showing you?

7. How can you be a better model of speaking life to those around you?

> "DAMAGING WORDS HAVE NO WINNERS; AFFIRMING WORDS HAVE NO LOSERS."

Chapter 7

HAUNTED BY THE PAST

Brethren, I do not count myself to have apprehended; but one thing I do, forgetting those things which are behind and reaching forward to those things which are ahead, I press toward the goal for the prize of the upward call of God in Christ Jesus.
—Philippians 3:13–14

She appeared to be one of the most optimistic, pleasant people I had ever met. She served faithfully in the church and was surrounded by lots of friends. When she called one day and asked to see me, I assumed she wanted to ask a question or two about the church's plans or her role in the future. Man, I couldn't have been more wrong. As soon as she sat down, she started weeping. She couldn't talk for several minutes. I thought she must have just heard some tragic news about a family member or friend. That wasn't it. Finally, she spoke through her sobs: "Pastor, I've been living a lie. I've been a phony." I knew there was a lot more to this confession, so I waited for her to continue. "My whole life I've tried to be someone I'm not. I wanted so much to be accepted that I did (and do) everything I can to make people like me."

I tried to console her: "They do like you. You're a delightful person."

She almost yelled, "But that's the problem! I'm not delightful. I'm a mess."

I paused for a few seconds and then said, "Tell me what you're thinking and feeling."

She poured out her story of growing up in a home filled with anger and intimidation from her mother and passive father. When she was nine years old, her parents divorced; she thought things would calm down, but her mother married another man who wouldn't stand up to her, and her father moved to another state. After telling me the details of her story, she came back to her present problem. "My entire life I've carried the weight of feeling unwanted, devalued, and alone. I hated being manipulated by my mother, but I now realize I've manipulated people to get them to like me. I'm sinning in the same way my mother sinned against me!" She burst into tears again.

She had been a faithful member of the church for many years. She was married and had two teenage sons. When I asked how they were doing, she started sobbing again. "I'm afraid I've done them irreparable harm! I feel so helpless...so ashamed."

She's not alone in her struggles. For many people the weight of past mistakes and painful memories feels impossible to shake. Some are victims, but others are perpetrators. They have to face the fact that their addictions, lies, selfishness, abuse, and crimes have left a trail of destruction. Regret, guilt, resentment, and shame can cloud every thought and interaction in the present. The way we respond determines whether we remain stuck in the past or experience healing and forgiveness and have the load lifted from our shoulders. This woman observed, "My past was like a giant octopus. Every time I tried to move forward, one of its tentacles grabbed me and held me back. How can I get away this time?"

It Makes Sense

Our brains are naturally wired to react quickly to threats. The amygdalae are two small clusters of nuclei near our temples. When we sense danger—real or perceived, often heightened by painful memories—these structures instantly go into action, automatically releasing stress hormones and triggering the mind and body into action. It's perfectly good and right when we see an oncoming car swerving toward us or when our toddler is about to fall off a slide, but those who have experienced recurring threats in childhood often kick into this gear when there's no actual danger. They feel they're constantly under threat, so these hormones continue to stimulate the self-defense response. Like a combat veteran ducking for cover at the sound of a loud noise, these people interpret many events as threats. The release of adrenaline keeps them on edge, their heart rates remain elevated, they have difficulty thinking clearly, and they may even have digestive problems. It's called "amygdala hijacking." This is the fight-or-flight reaction.

The problem is that our brains are wired to see change as a threat, so we stay stuck in our dysfunctional reactions. In our interpretation of events throughout our lives, we have constructed a powerful web of beliefs to protect ourselves and earn some peace and acceptance. New information—like the wonderful truth of our new identity as God's chosen, beloved, adopted children—seems to "bounce off the surface" because it doesn't fit with our carefully constructed belief systems. Psychologist Greg Lester explains it this way:

> [Our] beliefs are designed to operate independent of sensory data [sight, hearing, taste, touch, and smell]. In fact, the whole survival value of beliefs is based on their ability to persist in the face of contradictory evidence. Beliefs are not supposed to change easily or simply in response to disconfirming evidence. If they did, they would be virtually useless as tools for survival.
>
> When data and belief come into conflict, the brain does not automatically give preference to data. This is why beliefs—even bad beliefs, irrational beliefs, silly beliefs, or crazy beliefs—often don't die in the face of contradictory evidence. The brain…is extremely reticent to jettison its beliefs. Like an old soldier with an old gun who does not quite trust that the war is really over, the brain often refuses to surrender its weapon even though the data say it should.[14]

That's why some people, like the woman from the church, can read the Bible, sing God's praise, and serve faithfully but remain buried under the avalanche of previous, self-defeating beliefs. I'm not trying to be pessimistic, just realistic. This is why we need the Spirit of God to work deeply in our minds and hearts to transform us from the inside out, and that's why we need others in the body of Christ to love us so well that our long-held false beliefs can gradually erode and make room for more of God's love, forgiveness, and acceptance.

One of the wonders of modern science is the discovery that our brains don't stop growing and changing after childhood. Neuroplasticity is the brain's ability to adapt to change by creating new neurons and crafting new neural networks. Change is hard, but it's certainly possible.

Even Them

Before we knew him as the apostle Paul, he was Saul, the radical, zealous Pharisee. He was fiercely committed to God, and he saw Christ and His followers as a threat. His solution was to persecute them out of existence. On a trip to Damascus to capture and eliminate Christians there, Jesus appeared to him and changed his life forever. In three days of isolation he had plenty of time to think about how wrong he had been about Jesus, but instead of being trapped by guilt, he embraced God's grace, let go of his past, and stepped into his calling. His life shows us that our mistakes and sins don't have to define us. In his letter to the Christians in Philippi, he explained, "Brethren, I do not count myself to have apprehended; but one thing I do, forgetting those things which are behind and reaching forward to those things which are ahead, I press toward the goal for the prize of the upward call of God in Christ Jesus" (Philippians 3:13–14).

Nelson Mandela had a powerful sense of justice. Racial discrimination in South Africa was enshrined in its constitution, but Mandela and many others sought change. Nationwide strikes proved ineffective, so in 1962 he received military training so he could lead an armed uprising. He and ten others were arrested the following year and tried on charges of sabotage. Months later he testified in his defense, proclaiming, "I have fought against white domination, and I have fought against black domination. I have cherished the ideal of a democratic and free society in which all persons live together in harmony and with equal opportunities. It is an ideal which I hope to live for and to achieve. But if needs be, it is an ideal for which I am prepared to die."[15] He was convicted, sentenced to life in prison, and sent to the hard labor prison on Robben

Island. When the government dropped the ban on his political party, he was released from prison, still determined to end white minority rule in South Africa. He was elected president of his party, and in 1994 he was inaugurated as the nation's first democratically elected president.

When Mandela was in prison, he could have been hardened by the lack of progress in ending apartheid in South Africa. He could have become bitter and cynical, but he chose forgiveness. He didn't let his imprisonment and hard labor make him a prisoner of resentment. He used the experience to fuel the fight for unity and healing.

One of the most remarkable legacies of Mandela's leadership is the Truth and Reconciliation Commission, established by Mandela and Bishop Desmond Tutu to bring victims and perpetrators of racial violence together for forgiveness and understanding. The work of the commission began in 1994 and continues to this day:

> Through over 2,500 hearings, it allowed individuals to seek amnesty and listened to around 21,000 victims, with 2,000 bravely sharing their stories in public sessions. Operating under the Department of Justice and Constitutional Development, the TRC's recommendations are still being put into action. This includes compensating victims, creating appropriate memorials, offering medical support, aiding affected communities, and providing educational bursaries to descendants of apartheid-era victims. A crucial part of this effort involves locating and repatriating the remains of victims from the apartheid era, ensuring they are returned to their families.[16]

The apostle Paul and Mandela remind us that while we can't change the past, we can choose how we respond to it. We can let it weigh us down, or we can learn from it and move forward with a renewed sense of purpose. The past can be a prison or a classroom. When we open our hearts and trust God to work His grace into the recesses of our hearts, we can heal, forgive, and grow.

But Why?

It's not fair for a child to suffer a parent's abuse or neglect. It's not fair for people who love God to suffer. It's not fair for someone who has never smoked a cigarette to get lung cancer. But these and countless other injustices happen to us. The Scriptures don't tell us, "Quit whining and get over it!" No, the writers take us into the heart of the issue. No one wrestled with the problem of evil like Job. He complained,

> My heart is in turmoil and cannot rest; days of affliction confront me. I go about mourning, but not in the sun; I stand up in the assembly and cry out for help.
> —Job 30:27–28

The ethical and theological dilemma is as old as the writer of Job and as fresh as today's news of tragedy and heartache. It's classically summed up like this: If God is good, surely He wouldn't allow suffering; therefore, there must be some limitations of His sovereign power to secure goodness for His people. Or, if God does have complete sovereign power over everything, suffering surely shows that He doesn't care that bad things happen to people, so He is not good. But the mental, emotional, and spiritual struggle for us in the face of a crisis is not a philosophical debate. An answer to our question is intensely personal and necessary for our survival. Like Job's, our agony is very real, current, and devastating. In his commentary on Job, Francis Anderson observes:

> Evil is not always—not often!—punished in proportion to guilt; good is not always—not often!—rewarded in proportion to merit. The case of Job precipitates the test of faith in its severest form—the supremely righteous man who sustains the most extreme calamities. How can he, or anyone, continue to believe that God is right and fair in what He sometimes does to people? There can be no doubt that it is God, only God, who is responsible for all that happens to Job. It cannot be blamed on "Nature" or the Devil, for these are but His creatures.[17]

Job asks many questions, but he is never condemned by God for asking them. Some might self-righteously say, "Ours is not to reason why; ours is but to do or die," but God says to us, "Come, let us reason together." Almighty God is not surprised or offended by our questions—He invites them because they show we're pursuing Him.

Inside Out

Changing deeply held (and often inarticulate) beliefs is hard, but it's both possible and necessary if we're to live vibrant, faith-filled lives. Over the years, I've found several practices to be very helpful.

1. Accept God's forgiveness.

Living within the high walls of self-defense may have seemed completely reasonable and necessary when we were younger, but the strategy often has a negative side effect: We're so emotionally protective that we have difficulty accepting God's gift of forgiveness. Some of us feel so unworthy that we can't imagine God forgiving us. But we must remember that His gracious offer extends to every human being, even those who have been hit men for the mob!

Others of us wrestle with anger at injustice and blame God or other people for what happened. Blame shifting becomes an art and a sport! In John's first letter he explains, "If we say that we have no sin, we deceive ourselves, and the truth is not in us. If we confess our sins, He is faithful and just to forgive us our sins and to cleanse us from all unrighteousness" (1 John 1:8–9).

You may see yourself primarily as a victim, not a sinner. I understand this perception. Some of us have been cruelly treated, but healing involves being honest with God about the ways we've tried to manage our lives on our own. You may be a victim, but you're also a sinner in need of God's cleansing.

2. Renew your mind.

As Lester observed, it's very difficult to change beliefs, but it's possible. And reading a verse or two from time to time won't get the job done—we must saturate our minds and hearts with the Word of God. Resentment and shame may *feel* right in the moment, but they're poisons that will ultimately leave us withered, crippled, and bitter. The antidote is the Word—the written Word (the Bible) and the living Word (Jesus). Paul pointed back to the power of the gospel as our motivation to do the hard work of mental and spiritual transformation:

> I beseech you therefore, brethren, by the mercies of God, that you present your bodies a living sacrifice, holy, acceptable to God, which is your reasonable service. And do not be conformed to this world, but be transformed by the renewing of your mind, that you may prove what is that good and acceptable and perfect will of God.
>
> —ROMANS 12:1–2

Paul pleaded with his readers to look at the cross as the turning point in history and the defining point in their lives. Our minds are inundated by thousands of worldly messages every day. We have to be disciplined and diligent to replace those messages with what's "good and acceptable and perfect."

Education expert Zaretta Hammond notes, "The old adage we usually hear is that 'practice makes perfect.' Based on what we know about neuroplasticity and deliberate practice, we should rephrase that to read, 'practice makes permanent.' As you organize yourself for [the training she leads], remember that it is not about being perfect but about creating new neural pathways that shift your default cultural programming as you grow in awareness and skill."[18]

3. Grieve your losses.

Every emotional wound is a loss—the loss of innocence, safety, security, and identity—and we need to grieve our losses so they lose their grip on us. Grieving is hard work, and it takes time. We don't finish grieving abuse or abandonment in one good cry! I understand this can be extremely difficult—some of us feel uncomfortable bringing up the past. We want to just forget it, lock it in the closet, and never open the door. But that's not how life works. If we aren't honest about our wounds, they'll continue to shadow every moment of our lives. Find someone who has been down this road before, and lean on that person's experience, understanding, patience, and compassion. It may be difficult at first, but it'll be worth it.

4. Forgive those who hurt you.

Where do you find the courage and power to forgive those who hurt you? By drawing on the wealth of God's forgiveness for you. Paul taught that those who experience love can love others, and those who experience forgiveness forgive others:

> Therefore, as the elect of God, holy and beloved, put on tender mercies, kindness, humility, meekness, longsuffering; bearing with one another, and forgiving one another, if anyone has a complaint against another; even as Christ forgave you, so you also must do.
> —Colossians 3:12–13

Some say, "I can't forgive. It's not fair!" We have a God-given sense of justice and injustice, and we know someone has to pay. In the heat of the moment, revenge *seems* right, but just like resentment and shame, it ultimately destroys us. Lewis Smedes noted, "Vengeance is having a videotape planted in your soul that cannot be turned off. It plays the painful scene over and over again inside your mind.... And each time it plays, you feel the clap of pain again.... Forgiving turns off the videotape of pained memory. Forgiving sets you free."[19]

When Pastor R. T. Kendall taught the story of Joseph and related the passage at the end of Genesis when he told his brothers that he had forgiven them and they had nothing to fear, he explained, "You know that you've totally forgiven somebody when you don't have to tell what they did." That's a good gauge.

5. Share your story.

Isolation usually amplifies regrets and hurts. We need to share our stories, but we must choose the listener wisely. Find a mature, godly person who is known for wisdom and compassion. Most of us are willing to share only the surface truths at first, and that's understandable. As trust grows, vulnerability follows. One of the most powerful and important spiritual disciplines is confessing our sins to a trustworthy person. When we find the courage to share "that one thing we hoped no one would ever know about us," and the person doesn't laugh, mock, or run away, we experience a new depth of God's healing. James wrote, "Confess your trespasses to one another, and pray for one another, that you may be healed. The effective, fervent prayer of a righteous man avails much" (James 5:16). God has given us "one another" so we don't ever have to walk alone.

But what if you don't have someone in your life whom you trust to share your struggle with? First, be encouraged that you can still experience healing from sharing your story—even if it's not with another person right now. Many wise counselors throughout the years have taught the power of expression in healing—sometimes you just need to "get it out." If you don't have a trusted person in your life right now to share with, then find a way to express what's bottled up inside you. Write down your story in a journal, draw or paint a picture that represents your story, compose music that expresses the emotion of your experiences, or go for a walk and process out loud to yourself. Whatever method you choose to express your experiences, always end by taking time to find where Jesus was in your story. Ask Him to reveal the truth about who He is to you and who you are to Him.

Second, I encourage you to find a pastor at your church or a counselor who follows biblical guidance. Even if you may not know them personally, they can be a trusted source to encourage you and help you recognize God's truth in your story. Finally, prayerfully consider who *is* in your life right now. Is there someone who may be a trustworthy person you simply haven't considered before? Ask God to begin to reveal people in your life whom you can begin to trust, and start building that relationship by sharing small details with them.

6. Be tenacious.

Transforming our minds and restoring our souls is a lifelong journey (more on this in chapter 10). God often gives us flashes of insight and moments of clarity, but these bursts of growth are usually followed by months and years of letting these truths seep into the deepest parts of our hearts. Spiritual progress is more like a long hike in the mountains than a helicopter ride to the top. We need patience and tenacity to keep going, but along the way we'll see amazing vistas and meet wonderful travelers. Our futures are the product of the small but important choices we make each day. We can try to coast, but sooner or later we'll end up in the ditch.

For years or even decades many of us have avoided facing the truth about our painful pasts. It was easier to minimize ("It wasn't that bad"), excuse ("She couldn't help it"), or deny ("It didn't even happen"). But in His perfect timing God brings it to the forefront. To get our attention, He may use (*use*, not *cause*) an illness, marital conflict or divorce, depression, financial collapse, a wayward child, or any of a hundred other events. Each one is a wake-up call to see who we really are and what we really believe. In *A Grief Observed*, C. S. Lewis says that facing heartache is a test:

> God has not been trying an experiment on my faith or love in order to find out their quality. He knew it already. It was I who didn't. In this trial, He makes us occupy the dock [where the accused stands], the witness box, and the bench all at once. He always knew that my temple was a house of cards. His only way of making me realize the fact was to knock it down.[20]

7. Invest in others.

As you increasingly experience God's love, forgiveness, and healing, you'll have opportunities to share that wealth with others. Some of the most powerful ministers of God's grace are those who have fought hard to believe it applies to them. They have developed incredible compassion for those who are hurting and have powerful testimonies of God's forgiveness. Paul encouraged the believers in Galatia, "For you, brethren, have been called to liberty; only do not use liberty as an opportunity for the flesh, but through love serve one another. For all the law is fulfilled in one word, even in this: 'You shall love your neighbor as yourself'" (Galatians 5:13–14).

A Testimony of Grace

Many people have repeated the quote "Hurt people hurt people." That's true, but it's also true that loved people love people, graced people grace people, forgiven people forgive people, and healed people heal people. I have the greatest admiration for those who have suffered terribly—from their own sins or the sins of others—and have found God to be the source of immeasurable grace and power. They have a testimony of God's faithfulness that never grows old. Elisabeth Kübler-Ross, who wrote one of the definitive books on grief, observed:

> The most beautiful people we have known are those who have known defeat, known suffering, known struggle, known loss, and have found their way out of the depths. These persons have an appreciation, a sensitivity, and an understanding of life that fills them with compassion, gentleness, and a deep loving concern. Beautiful people do not just happen.[21]

When we do the work of grieving, forgiving, and healing, the past no longer has permission to haunt us. No, we can't just wish it away. We may have spent years in the prison of our past, and it takes time to adjust to the reality of our freedom. We can be sure, though, that God has the door open for us. When Isaiah wrote, he described Israel's current predicament (in chapters 1–39) and looked forward to a better future (in chapters 40–66). We can look forward to a better future too. The prophet's quotation of God's promise is true for us as well:

> Do not remember the former things, nor consider the things of old. Behold, I will do a new thing, now it shall spring forth; shall you not know it? I will even make a road in the wilderness and rivers in the desert.
> —Isaiah 43:18–19

That Moment

During my childhood I tried to cope with my father's brutal mistreatment—primarily of my mother but also of the kids. In order to survive, I built my own version of reality. I believed my mother's love would shield me so thoroughly that I wouldn't be affected by my father. And my father wasn't constantly mean and condemning. In the moments when he was pleasant around the house, came to my games, or showed some interest in what we were doing, I told myself his belligerence didn't bother me that much. I thought, "Other dads are just like him." I was "just fine"—at least that's what I told myself and anyone who asked. Intuitively, I sensed that if I called out my father's behavior, being honest would put my mom at risk, and I couldn't bear that. I had created a world where my mom and I could survive, but that world required half-truths and selective blindness. But when I looked in the mirror one day and saw someone who was too much like my dad, the excuses and rationalizations shattered. I came face-to-face with a painful reality.

Other people have very different turning point moments. Their families may have held an intervention, and they've gone to rehab. After detoxing for a few terrible days, their chemical crutches have crumbled, and they face choices about their future. For others, it might be the death of a child or spouse, a divorce, a health scare, a natural disaster, or something else. Stress comes in all sizes and shapes, and sometimes positive events like a marriage, promotion, or retirement can shake a person's foundation and prompt honest reflection.

Now that I'm on the other side of my moment looking in the mirror, I'm never shocked when people tell me horror stories about their sinful choices or how they've been victimized. My experience of God's kindness has dug a deep well of compassion for others who are struggling. Our experiences may be quite different, but that doesn't matter. I can listen, affirm truth, listen more, and provide the comfort and direction they need. And if God uses my story to touch one person and change that life, it's all worth it—that's what I told Tonia when we moved from Idaho to Mississippi. God has brought people from near and far to our church, not because I preach on healing past hurts every Sunday but because they sense I've been where they are and that I genuinely care about them.

When we look at nativity scenes at Christmas, they're always calm, serene, and loving. It's easy to forget the drama that happened only a few months earlier. Mary told her fiancé, Joseph, the utterly unbelievable story that she was pregnant, and the father was the Holy Spirit. I can imagine Joseph thinking, "Yeah, right. Can't you come up with a better story than that?" It took the appearance of an angel to assure him that she was telling the truth. But what would the neighbors say when they saw her stomach bump? How could he defend her when *he* hadn't even believed her at first? God put this couple in a very difficult situation, but it wasn't over. About two years later, when the wise men showed up and told Herod that a new king had been born, an angel warned Joseph and Mary, telling them to take Jesus to Egypt. Throughout the rest of His childhood Jesus was a refugee in a foreign land. When Jesus entered into the stage of His ministry when great crowds followed Him, some of those who doubted were His own family. Mark records, "When his family heard about this, they went to take charge of him, for they said, 'He is out of his mind'" (Mark 3:21, NIV). That had to hurt.

Thankfully, God touched their hearts. We see Mary at the cross (John 19:25), and His half-brother James became a leader in the early church and presided over the crucial Jerusalem Council. From His conception to His death Jesus suffered rejection, exile, and isolation. The writer to the Hebrews puts His experience in perspective for us: "For we do not have a High Priest who cannot sympathize with our weaknesses, but was in all points tempted as we are, yet without sin. Let us therefore come boldly to the throne of grace, that we may obtain mercy and find grace to help in time of need" (Hebrews 4:15–16). When you talk to Jesus about the pain of your past, He understands because He's been there.

Consider this:

1. Do you think the phrase "haunted by the past" is too strong? Why or why not?

2. How does the promise of neuroplasticity (see explanation in chapter 7) give us hope for real and lasting change?

3. What are some concrete steps we can take to prepare ourselves to respond to difficulties instead of reacting?

4. Pick two of the steps from the list under the heading "Inside Out," and write a plan for improvement:

   • Accept God's forgiveness.

   • Renew your mind.

   • Grieve your losses.

   • Forgive those who hurt you.

   • Share your story.

   • Be tenacious.

   • Invest in others.

5. Look again at Colossians 3:12–13. How does Paul describe the motivation and power to forgive those who have hurt us?

6. Who do you know who has "a testimony of grace"? What's attractive about that person?

> "WHEN WE OPEN OUR HEARTS AND TRUST GOD TO WORK HIS GRACE INTO THE RECESSES OF OUR HEARTS, WE CAN HEAL, FORGIVE, AND GROW."

CHAPTER 8

LET SETBACKS BECOME COMEBACKS

For a righteous man may fall seven times
and rise again, but the wicked shall fall by calamity.
—Proverbs 24:16

What's the difference? What is it about some people that they can fall flat on their faces and get up and go at it again, while others can't seem to find the strength to stand back up? It's not intelligence, talent, resources, or skills—it's attitude. One believes God can turn the setback into a comeback, but the other doesn't.

We love great stories, don't we? We talk about our favorite novels and movies, and we identify with the characters. In my opinion the greatest stories are those that tell of someone going through extreme difficulties to accomplish something noble and good. We feel the tension as the protagonist faces danger and death to save someone, and sometimes the hero dies to rescue the one he loves. During the twists and turns in

The Shift That Changes Everything

the plot, we agonize as things look hopeless, and we're amazed at the raw courage that brings a surprising resolution.

These stories of triumph aren't just on the screen or the page—we have the opportunity to live in the middle of a great story!

Contemporary Comebacks

Over four days in October 2004, the impossible became plausible and then inevitable. The Boston Red Sox's 2003 season ended in the American League Championship Series with an extra-inning loss to the Yankees. When the next season ended, the two teams were locked in the ALCS again. Red Sox fans hoped this was the year the Curse of the Bambino would finally be broken. Eighty-six years before, the owner of the Red Sox had sold his star, Babe Ruth (the Bambino), to the Yankees to fund one of his Broadway plays. The Red Sox had been world champions with Ruth; without him they were only ordinary—and they stayed ordinary for over eight long decades, with only the occasional flash of brilliance.

In game one the Yankees sprinted to an 8–0 lead. By the end of the game the Red Sox had brought it to within one run, but the Yankees held on for the win. The Yankees won the next two games, including a 19–8 drubbing in game three, for a commanding 3–0 lead in the series. No team in Major League Baseball history had ever come back from this deficit, so Boston fans were already thinking of the next year. In game four the Yankees had a one-run lead in the ninth inning and were ready to close out the best-of-seven series, but Boston's Dave Roberts was put in the game to run for Kevin Millar, who had walked. Everyone in the ballpark knew he was going to try to steal. Mariano Rivera, the greatest closing pitcher in the game, threw to first base several times to keep Roberts close, but on Rivera's first pitch to the plate, Roberts took off. He beat the throw to second and was in scoring position. A single hit by Bill Mueller brought Roberts home, and "Big Poppy" David Ortiz hit a home run in extra innings for the win. In game five the Red Sox again faced elimination in the late innings, but they tied the game and won again in the fourteenth inning. The Yankees still held a 3–2 lead in the series. Game six is famous for Red Sox pitcher Curt Schilling throwing seven strong innings with his right sock soaked in blood from an open ankle injury. The Sox won again. Now, with the series tied, all the momentum was on Boston's side. They won game seven handily, 10–3.

The Red Sox faced the outstanding St. Louis Cardinals team in the World Series, but the momentum from their miraculous comeback against the Yankees carried them to a sweep. They had done it. The curse was broken! It was one of the most amazing stories in baseball history.

Tiger Woods is in the small group of the greatest golfers of all time, but by 2017, injuries, four back surgeries, and personal struggles had eroded his skills. The unquestioned master of the game had fallen to number 1,199 in the world rankings. His fourteenth major tournament title had been in 2008—almost a decade earlier. Many believed his run was over, but Woods wasn't one of them. At the Masters that April in Augusta, Georgia, Woods played better than he had in years. When the fourth and final round started, he was two strokes behind Francesco Molinari. The short but treacherous twelfth hole cost Molinari the lead when his tee shot splashed into the water in front of the green. Woods birdied three of the next four holes and had a two-shot lead going into the eighteenth hole. He needed only a bogey for the win, and that's what he got, "sending the patrons at Augusta National into a frenzy.... Tiger pierced the sky with both fists when the ball found the bottom of the cup. He let out a primal scream as the weight of trying to achieve what some believed to be impossible was lifted off his shoulders. Then a large smile stretched across his face as the reality of what he had accomplished started to set in."[22] He walked off the green and hugged his children. It was one of the greatest comebacks in sports history, but it wouldn't be his last.

By 2021 Woods had won every major tournament multiple times and dominated the game like no one since Jack Nicklaus two decades earlier. But in February of that year, his car was going too fast down a winding road when it crashed and careened into the bushes. He suffered multiple serious injuries, including fractures to his right leg and ankle. He underwent extensive surgery and a long rehab. During that time, few people thought he would ever play competitive golf again, but still, he returned to the tour, playing in the 2022 Masters. Even though he navigates injuries to this day, he continues to compete.

These stories remind us that every setback gives us the opportunity for a dramatic comeback. Most of us have had some kind of blow that looked like the end—in our careers, our finances, our faith, our health, or our most important relationships. Life's most important lessons often come disguised as setbacks. And the difference between a setback becoming a permanent definition or a thrilling comeback is our *attitude*. Pessimism leaves us in despair, but optimism finds opportunities in the darkest times. Failure isn't final unless we decide to quit.

Let Setbacks Become Comebacks

Setbacks shape our character more fully and profoundly than success because we have to dig deep to find hidden resources of purpose, strength, and motivation. Look at setbacks as detours, not dead ends. Some people are surprised when they experience difficulties, but I don't think they've read the Bible very carefully! God hasn't promised an easy life for those who follow Him, but He has promised to provide His presence, pardon, purpose, and power as we walk with Him through good times and bad. Solomon reminds us of this principle:

> For a righteous man may fall seven times and rise again, but the wicked shall fall by calamity.
> —Proverbs 24:16

If you'll bear with me, I want to tell one more baseball story. Jim Morris was a thirty-five-year-old high school science teacher, a father of three, and the coach of the school's baseball team in Brownwood, Texas. To motivate his team, he made a deal that if they managed to win the district championship, he'd try out for a major-league team. He thought it was a safe bet, but his team went on a winning streak, became champs of the district, and earned a spot in the state playoffs. True to his word, Morris signed up for a tryout with a bunch of kids almost half his age, and he impressed the scouts by throwing ninety-eight miles an hour. (In case you don't know, that's really fast!) The Tampa Bay Devil Rays signed him, and only three months later he was picked from the minors to join the club to face the Texas Rangers in Arlington. In the bottom of the eighth inning with the Rays behind 6–1, the manager called him out of the bullpen to pitch to one batter. The man at the plate had been an All-Star, so this was a challenge for Morris.

His first two fastballs were swings and misses, the third was fouled off, and the fourth produced a weak swing and a miss for the third strike. "One batter, one out, one memory to last a lifetime. That his family was able to be there for it just made it all the more special."

You may have heard of this story because it was made into a successful movie, *The Rookie*, starring Dennis Quaid. A few years after the debut, Quaid commented, "The movie is all about gratitude," he said. "Jimmy and I are still close friends. He came to my mother's funeral two years ago....A lot of people wouldn't be able to handle all of [the attention from the movie]. But I think Jimmy had learned humility and how tentative everything is. It made him grateful. He's a fine human being. And I ought to know, because I played him!"

Looking back on the genesis of all this, Morris remembers, "It was all because of a bet with a group of kids. If it hadn't been for those kids, I would never have tried."[23]

Joni Eareckson Tada grew up in a family of athletes. Her father participated as a wrestler in the Olympic Games, and she rode horses, hiked, swam, and played tennis. In the summer of 1967, when she was seventeen, she dove into Chesapeake Bay but misjudged the depth of the water. She fractured vertebrae in her neck and was paralyzed from the neck down. In an instant her life irrevocably changed. During two years of rehab she struggled with depression, anger, suicidal thoughts, and doubts about the goodness of God. In the middle of it all, an occupational therapist taught Joni to paint with a brush held between her teeth, and she began selling her art. Using voice-recognition software, Joni has written more than forty books. Her autobiography was made into a movie: *A Step Further*. She started a nonprofit organization called Joni and Friends and

Let Setbacks Become Comebacks

has served on many government councils for disabilities. She's an accomplished public speaker and serves on the boards of numerous organizations. She is known for her relentless optimism and rich wisdom born from tragic adversity. Reflecting on her experience, she observes, "Nothing is a surprise to God; nothing is a setback to His plans; nothing can thwart His purposes; and nothing is beyond His control. His sovereignty is absolute. Everything that happens is uniquely ordained by God. Sovereignty is a weighty thing to ascribe to the nature and character of God. Yet if He were not sovereign, He would not be God. The Bible is clear that God is in control of everything that happens."[24]

When we hit rough patches and need some encouragement to take the next step, we often turn to Romans 8:28: "And we know that all things work together for good to those who love God, to those who are the called according to His purpose." In his book, *Into the Heart of Romans*, New Testament scholar N. T. Wright suggests a slightly different translation that clarifies God's offer: "We know, in fact, that God works all things together for good *with those who love him*, who are called according to his purpose." It's not that things *somehow* work out for good but that "God is our collaborator. God works with and through 'those who love him.'"[25] In other words, God has given us the honor and the responsibility to partner with Him in the great kingdom enterprise. The world sees our commitment to Christ most clearly when they see us trust Him in the midst of difficulties.

In the Scriptures

The Bible is filled with stories again and again of people suffering tragic setbacks but finding the courage to make a comeback. Saul's entire army was terrified of the giant Goliath. In warfare of the day, each side often sent out a champion to fight one-on-one, and the winner's side made the other army their slaves. The situation looked hopeless—until an overlooked shepherd boy told the king, "I'll do it!"

God told Jonah to take the message of hope to Nineveh, the capital of Assyria, the nation that had destroyed the ten tribes of the Northern Kingdom of Israel. Jonah didn't want the Assyrians to repent and experience God's forgiveness; he wanted them to pay for their brutality! Instead of booking a trip to Nineveh, he hopped on a ship going in the opposite direction. God didn't take no for an answer, so He had a storm batter the ship until Jonah went overboard to save the rest of the crew. To make matters worse, he was swallowed by a whale (which they called "a big fish") and was carried to shore smelling like half-digested seafood. I don't think he looked triumphant when he walked into Nineveh to preach God's words, but thousands repented. It was a stunning comeback for the people of Nineveh and an equally surprising one for the reluctant evangelist.

The prodigal in Jesus' parable threw his inheritance away on "wild living," and the only job this Jewish man could find was feeding pigs in the "far country." But his father didn't give up on him—he welcomed his son with open arms and restored him.

The widow of Zarephath and her son were dying of hunger during a prolonged famine. When Elijah came to town, he asked her for a drink of water and a piece of bread. She explained that she was preparing for the end: "As the Lord your God lives, I do not have bread, only a handful of flour in a bin, and a little oil in a jar; and see, I am gathering a couple of sticks that I may go in and prepare it for myself and my son, that we may eat it, and die" (1 Kings 17:12). Elijah wasn't preparing to die, and he wasn't willing to let this woman and her son die. He told her to make a small cake for him and them, and he promised, "For thus says the LORD God of Israel: 'The bin of flour shall not be used up, nor shall the jar of oil run dry, until the day the LORD sends rain on the earth'" (1 Kings 17:14). I wonder what she was thinking when she heard that promise? Whatever her questions may have been, she did as Elijah instructed, and the flour and oil were miraculously replenished until the rains came again.

But my favorite story of a comeback in the Scriptures is Peter's. He was the leader of the disciples, the one who often spoke for all of them. As the week after the triumphal entry progressed and Jesus faced opposition from the establishment, Peter thought Jesus was ready to be the new king. At the Last Supper, when Jesus announced that one of them would betray Him, Peter insisted, "Even if all are made to stumble, yet I will not be."

Jesus told him the hard truth: "Assuredly, I say to you that today, even this night, before the rooster crows twice, you will deny Me three times."

But Peter doubled down: "If I have to die with You, I will not deny You!" (Mark 14:29–31).

A few hours later, when Jesus was arrested in the Garden of Gethsemane, Peter swung a sword and cut off the ear of the high priest's servant. (He was a fisherman, not a soldier, so his aim wasn't very good!) Jesus put the ear back on and was led away to be tried by the religious leaders.

Outside, where the trial was happening, Peter listened. One of the high priest's servant girls noticed him warming himself by a charcoal fire and recognized him as a follower of Jesus (Mark 14:66–67). Peter reacted, "I neither know nor understand what you are saying." A rooster crowed (v. 68).

Peter left and walked out to the porch, but the girl saw him again and identified him as one of the disciples. Again, Peter denied knowing Jesus (v. 69). Later, others recognized him and could tell he wasn't from Jerusalem because of his accent: "Surely you are one of them; for you are a Galilean, and your speech shows it" (v. 70).

This time Peter "began to curse and swear, 'I do not know this Man of whom you speak!'" (v. 71). A second rooster crowed, and Peter realized what he'd done. He wept bitter tears (v. 72).

Peter, the group's leader, had betrayed Jesus—not to the threatening Pharisees or the fierce Roman soldiers, but to a girl and some people he didn't know. It looked as if it was over for him, but when Jesus came out of the tomb, an angel told the women who came to anoint Jesus' body with spices, "He is risen! He is not here. See the place where they laid Him. But go, tell His disciples—and Peter—that He is going before you into Galilee; there you will see Him, as He said to you" (Mark 16:6–7). The angel (and Jesus) wanted Peter to know he was still wanted.

Sometime later Peter and others were fishing in the Sea of Galilee. They fished all night but caught nothing. Early the next morning a man appeared on the beach and yelled for them to drop their nets again. They brought in a huge catch! In that moment, Peter realized it was Jesus. He put on his outer garment and jumped into the water to get to Jesus as soon as possible. When the disciples made it to the beach, they saw that Jesus had prepared a charcoal fire and was cooking fish and bread. After breakfast Jesus asked Peter three times, "Do you love Me?" and each time, Peter replied, "Yes, Lord; You know that I love You."

Two elements of this conversation stand out to me. First, of course, Peter had denied Jesus three times, so Jesus let him affirm his love three times. And second, John makes the point that Jesus had prepared a charcoal fire, the same kind Peter had stood by the night he denied Jesus. Experts say that smell is one of the most powerful sensory memories. That morning on the beach Jesus took Peter back to his worst moment when he denied Him, not to crush him with shame but to show him that his worst sin is fully known and completely forgiven. A couple of weeks later, who was the disciple who spoke to the crowd in Jerusalem at Pentecost? Yeah, it was Peter, the comeback kid. Who is the hero of the story? We naturally think of Peter hanging in there through his most horrible moments and being restored, but it was Jesus who loved Peter in spite of his betrayal, restored him, and used him in a mighty way to launch a worldwide movement. Jesus is the real hero of the story.

Of course, the most amazing comeback story of all time is Jesus' resurrection. For three years He had loved, healed, and taught, but He was often reviled and rejected. In the supreme act of love, He endured false accusations, torture, and a horrific public execution, putting Himself in our place to do for us what we couldn't do for ourselves. No one conceived a dead Messiah. They expected Jesus to throw the Romans out and become the Davidic king, but He died the death reserved for the worst criminals of the day. His followers went to bed that night thinking they'd just witnessed the worst event in the history of the world, but again, they misunderstood Him. Three days later the earth shook and

Jesus came out of the tomb in His glorified, victorious body. The comeback was complete—one that reminds us that nothing is beyond the touch of God's love and power.

Augustine lived at the turn of the fifth century. He had lived a life of radical self-indulgence, but when Jesus changed his heart, he became one of the most influential believers in history. He had a deep grasp of the irony in the life of Jesus— defeats were actually victories, and limitations only revealed His glory. He wrote:

> Man's maker was made man that He, Ruler of the stars, might nurse at His mother's breast; that the Bread might hunger, the Fountain thirst, the Light sleep, the Way be tired on his journey; that the Truth might be accused of false witness, the Teacher be beaten with whips, the Foundation be suspended on wood; that Strength might grow weak; that the Healer might be wounded; that Life might die.[26]

Have you suffered some setbacks? Don't despair. Don't allow them to tank your attitude and tempt you into giving up! God hasn't finished with you. Look for what God wants to do in you or teach you as you navigate these unexpected losses or defeats. The more you continue to look for God at work and maintain an attitude of faith and hope, the more you position yourself for the most incredible comeback.

Consider this:

1. What are your favorite novels or movies?
2. What do you like about them?
3. Who are the heroes?
4. What risk do they take for others?

Let Setbacks Become Comebacks

5. What real comeback stories inspire you? (It doesn't have to be about baseball!)

6. Describe a time when you faced a significant setback.

7. What was your initial reaction?

8. Was there a turning point that made it a comeback?

9. What lessons did you learn from the experience?

10. What comeback stories in the Bible inspire you? Explain your answer.

11. Who do you know who is experiencing a setback right now? How can you help that person have a "comeback attitude"?

> "SETBACKS SHAPE OUR CHARACTER MORE FULLY AND PROFOUNDLY THAN SUCCESS BECAUSE WE HAVE TO DIG DEEP TO FIND HIDDEN RESOURCES OF PURPOSE, STRENGTH, AND MOTIVATION."

CHAPTER 9

A NEW PAIR OF GLASSES

"The lamp of the body is the eye. If therefore your eye is good, your whole body will be full of light. But if your eye is bad, your whole body will be full of darkness. If therefore the light that is in you is darkness, how great is that darkness!"

—MATTHEW 6:22–23

Perception doesn't necessarily determine *what* we see but *how* we see. Our concept of what's real and true determines our attitude. If we believe people don't care, God has abandoned us, and we're on our own, we won't trust Him or others. We'll see every interaction as a manipulative threat. As we've seen in previous chapters, some of us will do anything and everything we can to earn the love we long for; others try to dominate people so they can't be hurt by them; and some devolve into self-pity and hopelessness, using substances or behaviors to distract themselves from the painful truth.

The Shift That Changes Everything

Our perspective determines how we interpret events and interactions. If we see a different truth when we look through our spiritual and emotional lenses—that God is good, loving, and sovereign—we have confidence that He has our best interests at heart even when circumstances go haywire. Every element of our lives is shaped by our ability to see clearly. Solomon observed, "For as he thinks in his heart, so is he" (Proverbs 23:7). Don't we think with our minds? Yes, but Solomon is getting to something more important: The heart is the seat of reflection where we filter what our senses tell us. Our hearts do more than observe life; they tell us what's real and what's not, who's trustworthy and who isn't, and whether fear or faith is the reasonable response.

My mother's consistent love and "courage under fire" were the most important factors in giving me an optimistic attitude. If she could be positive, compassionate, and kind in the face of the barrage of false accusations, then surely I could look for the good instead of dwelling on the bad. If Mom could do it, I could do it. It wasn't a momentary flash of insight; it was seeing my mother respond with grace and truth day after day, year after year. As I watched her bear with my father and endure his contempt, I absorbed her strength, honesty, and kindness. Each of these scenes was excruciating to observe, but I was amazed as she found the inner reserves to avoid falling into bitterness, hatred, and self-absorption.

The things I gleaned from my mother, I want to pay forward to the lives of Tonia, our children, our neighbors, the people at our church, and everyone I meet—even if only for a few moments. I'm the "half-full" guy, not the "half-empty" guy. No matter how bleak the situation may be, I look for the positives. Sometimes I have to dig pretty hard to find them, but they're always there. Tonia's father used to say, "If you put Ted in a desert, he'll find an oasis."

A positive attitude doesn't shield me from "real life" happening. I still experience disappointments, disagreements, and disasters, but God has given me the ability to choose a hopeful perspective in all of them.

Light and Darkness

People lack perception for one of two reasons: They're either ignorantly blind or willfully blind. Ignorant blindness results from a lack of experience and is overcome by every means of learning, particularly personal experience. Children touch a hot stove until they feel enough heat to teach them a valuable lesson. Adolescents often make less-than-genius choices because they're experimenting with their limits, and they learn from the consequences. Some of us gain perception by observing the consequences others experience—both pleasant and painful. Many of us only become perceptive, however, when we experience the consequences firsthand.

The second reason people lack perception is a much more difficult problem: willful ignorance. They don't see because they don't want to see. In the legal world it "occurs when someone intentionally keeps themselves unaware of facts that would render them liable or implicated in a wrongdoing."[27]

More broadly, willful ignorance is a defense to avoid any kind of painful responsibility.

"Is your husband drinking again?"
"I don't think so."
"What you said hurt my feelings."
"I didn't mean it."
"Your work isn't good enough."

"I had no idea."

"I heard your son got arrested."

"Maybe so. I don't ask too many questions."

These responses may sometimes be honest and true, but you get the idea. We can be masters of avoiding hard truths.

In His most famous sermon, Jesus told the crowd, "The lamp of the body is the eye. If therefore your eye is good, your whole body will be full of light. But if your eye is bad, your whole body will be full of darkness. If therefore the light that is in you is darkness, how great is that darkness!" (Matthew 6:22–23).

He used the metaphor of eyesight to illustrate the concept of perception. When our sight is clear, we can see everything—the good, the bad, and the ugly—and respond appropriately to everyone. A snapshot of what this means is found in Paul's letter to the Christians in Thessalonica:

> Now we exhort you, brethren, warn them that are unruly, comfort the feebleminded, support the weak, be patient toward all men.
>
> —1 Thessalonians 5:14, KJV

But if we lack clear eyesight about everyone and everything in our lives, we'll stumble around like someone bumping into furniture during a storm at night when the lights go out. It's interesting that Jesus gives one more statement to emphasize the contrast between clear and cloudy perception: "If therefore the light that is in you is darkness, how great is that darkness!" He's saying, "Watch out! This affects everything!" And, in fact, it does.

NEGATIVITY BIAS

For a variety of reasons, many people live with a negativity bias. It's defined as our bent to "attend to, learn from, and use negative information far more than positive information."[28] When these people enter a roomful of people, they wonder who is out to get them. When they attempt a project, they focus on what can go wrong. When they're alone and quiet, their resentment and regret bubble to the top of their consciousness. In virtually every situation, they see what's wrong (or what can go wrong) more than what's right.

When we read the story of God liberating His people from Egypt and providing for them in the wilderness, we marvel at God's patience and provision—but that's not how those people saw the experience! After they saw God's awesome presence on Sinai and Moses had brought the tablets down to them, they began their journey toward the Promised Land. The ark of the covenant went before them, and the cloud was above them. They were living in the midst of a miracle! But after only three days they complained. They were so upset that they wept and pleaded with Moses, "Who will give us meat to eat? We remember the fish which we ate freely in Egypt, the cucumbers, the melons, the leeks, the onions, and the garlic; but now our whole being is dried up; there is nothing at all except this manna before our eyes!" (Numbers 11:4–6). Yeah, they had food in Egypt, because they were slaves! And they lived on a subsistence diet, not the Michelin star dining they remembered! It's ironic that their negativity bias caused them to reinterpret the 430 years of grueling labor as slaves as a *pleasant* experience. At that moment, they couldn't see God's power or provision, or the big-picture perspective of God leading them into the land promised to their forefather Abraham. All they saw was their immediate needs, and they couldn't bring themselves to believe that the God who had already shown Himself in power in the plagues, the crossing of the Red Sea, the destruction of Pharaoh's army, and the fire and smoke on Sinai could be trusted to provide for them that day.

What is this about? Why are some people predisposed to being negative? Some develop a defensive mindset from painful childhood experiences. When they grow up, get married, have children, and pursue their careers, all the positives are quickly washed away in a flood of what-ifs, if-onlys, and what-abouts.

The news we watch on the television or read online is slanted much more toward the reporting of tragic and threatening events, so people with a negativity bias feel validated in thinking the world is going to hell and "the other side" is out to get them. Leaders who demand performance with very little affirmation reinforce the belief that "nothing I do is good enough."

I'm not suggesting that we shouldn't be analytical. Accurate perception is vital if we want to live God-honoring lives. Jesus didn't have "happy thoughts" about how the Pharisees used people for personal gain instead of loving them. He spoke the hard truth to call them to repentance. When Jesus described the Father's love for repentant sinners in the parable of the Prodigal Son, a group of Pharisees listened in and condemned Jesus for caring for "sinners." While the main character in the story is the younger brother, remember the father who went out to the angry, self-righteous older brother and invited him to come to the feast of salvation? The older brother was invited to repent, but he refused. It's always Jesus' hope that reproof will lead to repentance. The Bible—from Genesis to Revelation—contains rebukes, warnings, and correctives, but the negatives found in the Bible and from the mouth of Jesus point us to the infinite goodness of God and His grace poured out on sinners like us.

From Outside

There are so many "one another" passages in the New Testament because God wants to emphasize the vital connections among us. We're part of a body, with Christ as the head. We can't grow into mature believers without the input and encouragement of other Christians.

When Jesus appeared to Paul on the road to Damascus, he was blinded. The men with him led him by the hand to Damascus. For three days he couldn't see and he didn't eat or drink. He may have wondered if he would ever see again, but God led Ananias to Paul. Understandably, he wasn't eager to meet with the guy who had been capturing and persecuting Christians, but he obeyed God's command. When Ananias arrived where Paul was staying, he put his hands on Paul and said, "Brother Saul, the Lord Jesus, who appeared to you on the road as you came, has sent me that you may receive your sight and be filled with the Holy Spirit." Luke tells us, "Immediately there fell from his eyes something like scales, and he received his sight at once; and he arose and was baptized" (Acts 9:17–18). Paul began to see—not just Ananias and the room he was in but the purposes of God and his role in them. The transformation from a persecutor to a disciple required diligent study, prayer, and more interactions with believers. He taught and wrote what he was learning, and he mentored young leaders. We seldom see Paul without close companions in the rest of Luke's account.

THE SHIFT THAT CHANGES EVERYTHING

David was "a man after God's own heart," but he was also a first-class sinner! As king, he sent his army out to fight the Philistines. He should have been at the head of his forces, but he stayed back in Jerusalem. One day he saw a beautiful woman, Bathsheba, bathing on a rooftop nearby, and his lust overpowered his good sense. He sent for her, had sex with her, and, when he learned that she was pregnant, conspired to kill her husband, Uriah (who had been one of David's "mighty men" when he needed all the help he could get while fleeing from King Saul!). This was the betrayal of a friend, the friend's wife, and a nation, but since Uriah was dead, no one needed to know. It was willful blindness.

God sent the prophet Nathan to David, and he told the king a story about a rich man taking advantage of a poor man who owned a lamb. David was outraged at the story and said, "As the LORD lives, the man who has done this shall surely die!"

Nathan told him, "You are the man!" (2 Samuel 12:5–7).

Nathan pronounced God's judgment on David, and David no longer tried to hide his sin. Nathan assured him of God's forgiveness, but he would still suffer the consequences of his actions. We don't know how long David lived the lie that nothing was wrong, but he must have constructed an elaborate story to convince people (and himself) that life could go on without paying a price. It took the voice of a prophet to bring him to the painful truth.

Balaam was a prophet—of the worst kind. Balak, the king of the Moabites, wanted to push God's people away from his land during their Exodus to the Promised Land. He hired Balaam to curse Israel, but the prophet needed God's permission. Of course, God doesn't grant permission to curse the people He's blessed. Balak was angry at Balaam's delays and excuses, so he sent officials to offer more money for the curse. The price was right, so Balaam saddled his donkey and went with some officials toward Moab. On the road, God sent an angel to block their path. The donkey veered off the road to avoid the angel (which Balaam couldn't see). He beat the donkey, and they kept going. The angel then stood on the road between two steep sides. The donkey tried to avoid the angel by going close to one of the walls, crushing Balaam's foot. He still had enough strength to beat the donkey again. Then, the angel stood where the road was even more narrow, and the donkey lay down on the path, prompting a third beating.

"Then the LORD opened the mouth of the donkey, and she said to Balaam, 'What have I done to you, that you have struck me these three times?'"

Apparently unfazed by the animal talking to him, Balaam answered his donkey, "Because you have abused me. I wish there were a sword in my hand, for now I would kill you!"

The donkey defended itself, and then, Balaam's perception suddenly became much clearer: He saw the angel! The angel rebuked the prophet, and Balaam offered to turn back. The angel told him to keep going with Balak's officials, but "only the word that I speak to you, that you shall speak."

When Balaam, his donkey, and the officials met Balak, the prophet told the king that he would only say what God, through the angel, had told him to say. After the king built seven altars and offered seven bulls and seven rams for sacrifice, Balaam left to be alone. There, God told him to speak multiple blessings over Israel. It was the reverse of the curse! (Numbers 22–24).

Most of us are familiar with the story of Helen Keller, the woman who was born blind and deaf but learned to read, write, and speak. She was the first person with those disabilities to earn a Bachelor of Arts degree and became an advocate for people with disabilities. Many of us may not know "the rest of the story." When Helen's parents asked for help with their daughter, Anne Sullivan stepped into her life. Anne taught her to communicate by first spelling words into her hand, a breakthrough that led to Helen's ability to communicate with people far beyond her limited environment. Anne remained her steadfast friend, mentor, teacher, and interpreter until she died in 1936. Mark Twain called Anne a "miracle worker." What drove Anne to see potential in Helen when others saw only a pitiful, disabled girl? In her autobiography, Helen quotes Anne: "You cannot touch the clouds, you know; but you feel the rain and know how glad the flowers and the thirsty earth are to have it after a hot day. You cannot touch love either; but you feel the sweetness that it pours into everything. Without love, you would not be happy or want to play."[29]

Accepting Reality

I've learned to appreciate the courage and kindness of people who take the initiative to tell me things I may not want to hear. These people aren't my enemies; they're my trusted friends. Like Ananias, Nathan, and Balaam's donkey, God has given them an important role in my life. In the same way, God has given me that role in others' lives. I don't take it lightly. I can imagine how much prayer and preparation went into Ananias' meeting with Paul and Nathan's carefully worded story to David.

If we truly love people, we'll tell them the truth. We need to think, pray, and consider the best way to speak that truth, but love demands we find a way to speak up. Solomon noted:

A New Pair of Glasses

> Open rebuke is better than love carefully concealed. Faithful are the wounds of a friend, but the kisses of an enemy are deceitful.
> —Proverbs 27:5–6

When someone loves us enough to tell us the truth, metaphorically handing us a new pair of glasses, we're often shocked and embarrassed by what we see—and what we've failed to see for so long. We may not walk around assuming our vision of life and God is limited and flawed, but it is. We might think, "If I could just walk with Jesus like the disciples, I'd have it all together." Really? They were willing to follow Him, but they were as dense as fence posts! Willful blindness is much more comfortable—until it isn't. A friend of ours leads a support group for survivors of various kinds of abuse. He tells them, "You may have come because your marriage is falling apart, your kids are a mess, you've been depressed for a long time, or you're drinking or using drugs to numb the pain, or for some other reason, but there's really only one reason people walk through the door: desperation. People seek help only when they've given up on their own resources."

Have you been there?

Are you there now?

Do you know someone who is?

Far too many people who have trusted in Jesus see Him through the dark glasses of despair. "God may care about other people and work in their lives," they grimace, "but not me." Yes, we suffer heartache. Yes, we get knocked down. But God is still loving, kind, compassionate, powerful, and faithful. Earlier we looked at Paul's ruthless realism and persistent hope in 2 Corinthians 4; I want to focus on one part of the passage. After he says that no amount or kind of suffering can shatter his hopeful attitude, Paul describes the source of his hope: "always carrying about in the body the dying of the Lord Jesus, that the life of Jesus also may be manifested in our body" (2 Corinthians 4:10).

What gives us tenacious hope in the middle of difficulties? What puts love in our hearts and strength in our souls? It's the death and resurrection of Jesus. When we're "always carrying about in the body the dying of Jesus," we're reflecting often and always on the sacrifice He made for us. If His love is that deep, He certainly won't ever desert us or forsake us. If God had a bright future for Jesus after the brutal cruelty of the cross, surely God has something for us after we face our problems. Shockingly, in his letter to the Ephesians, Paul taught that the spiritual power available to us today, right now, is "according to the working of His mighty power which He worked in Christ when He raised Him from the dead and seated Him at His right hand in the heavenly places, far above all principality and power and might and dominion, and every name that is named, not only in this age but also in that which is to come" (Ephesians 1:19–21). You and I can live in resurrection power!

An optimistic, hopeful attitude isn't based on the DNA of a good personality, and it's not dependent on everything going well all the time. It doesn't rest on the approval and applause of others, and it's not the product of position or power. Hope—real hope—comes from our deep, rich grasp of the gospel of grace, so much so that our hearts are filled to overflowing. When we're convinced that "neither death nor life, nor angels nor principalities nor powers, nor things present nor things to come, nor height nor depth, nor any other created thing, shall be able to separate us from the love of God which is in Christ

A New Pair of Glasses

Jesus our Lord" (Romans 8:38–39), we'll find God faithful in every situation.

Consider this:

1. How would you define and describe ignorant blindness and willful blindness?

2. Do insight and perception necessarily give us a negativity bias? Why or why not?

3. In your life, who has loved you enough to tell you the truth when you didn't want to hear it?

4. How did you respond?

5. What difference has it made in the long run?

6. Do you believe that the only (or at least the primary) reason people change is desperation? Explain your answer.

7. Paraphrase 2 Corinthians 4:11. How does the sacrificial death and resurrection power of Jesus give you courage to face the difficulties in your life?

> "I STILL EXPERIENCE DISAPPOINTMENTS, DISAGREEMENTS, AND DISASTERS, BUT GOD HAS GIVEN ME THE ABILITY TO CHOOSE A HOPEFUL PERSPECTIVE IN ALL OF THEM."

Chapter 10

THE LIFELONG JOURNEY

> But we were gentle among you, just as a nursing mother cherishes her own children. So, affectionately longing for you, we were well pleased to impart to you not only the gospel of God, but also our own lives, because you had become dear to us.
> —1 Thessalonians 2:7-8

If I'd seen my mother respond positively to my father's belligerence only one time, it wouldn't have made much of a dent in my life perspective. Seeing her incredible blend of honesty about the abuse yet optimism about the future, lived out day after day during my childhood, showed me that a positive attitude is not only possible; it's *essential*.

Someone asked if my children have picked up my tenacious optimism. I laughed and explained, "Yes, they have. They would tell you that one word was never spoken in our home:

the word *can't*. It wasn't allowed. The simple elimination of this word forced them to look for solutions, not excuses."

My daughter Kristin has a carbon copy of my outlook on life—the same drive to make a difference and the same perspective of finding something good in every situation. In her home, her example is making a difference in her three children. My other children have absorbed my perspective too, but Kristin is the most like me in that way.

While my kids saw me every day, most of the people in our church only see and hear me once a week. When they come for the first time and stay for a month or so, some of them are skeptical of my optimism. They assume it can't be true. But more times than I can count, people have come forward during an invitation and told me, "Pastor Ted, now I get it. I understand why you're so excited about the Lord and optimistic that following Him is a bright light in our darkest times." (Most of them didn't tell me they had thought I was out of touch with reality before that moment, but that's what they meant.) I wouldn't take a million dollars in place of their genuine heart changes.

Over the years, some people who heard me preach relentless hope wrote me off to the people who brought them: "Pastor Ted is just a used-car salesman." I'm thrilled when the Spirit of God convinces them that all the promises of God are "yes and amen!" They may have come with a concept of God as harsh and condemning so they could never measure up, or distant and unconcerned with their hopes and hurts. When they begin to grasp the wonder of God's infinite love, extravagant sacrifice, and awesome presence and power, they may think I wasn't positive *enough*!

Not long ago a man came up to me after church and said, "Pastor, when I started coming a year ago, I thought you were a phony—nobody can be that positive all the time! But after watching you for a year, I can see you're authentic. That's who you are, and it's making a difference in me."

Positivity Principles

Over the years, as I've thought, talked, prayed, and preached about ruthless optimism to claim the promises of God, some principles have crystallized in my thinking. I've already shared a few of these, but it's helpful to put them in one place.

1. Managing your attitude is a lifelong pursuit, not a single decision. A single decision can set the course for your life, but it must be followed up with countless more decisions to create a cohesive, permanent pattern.

2. Challenges will continually arise, testing your attitude in every stage of life. The tests to find the good in adversity are different when we're adolescents than when we're the parents of adolescents—or the grandparents of adolescents.

3. Growth never stops. Having a hopeful, can-do attitude is a daily, intentional choice. We learn and grow more from adversity than when things are going smoothly.

4. Consistency is key. Yesterday's success or failure doesn't dictate today's mindset.

5. Embrace seasons of change. Your attitude will need to grow and adapt to each new season. Don't

be surprised when you react to difficulty with resentment or woe is me, but be honest about how you're reacting, ask God for a fresh sense of wisdom and insight, and choose faith again.

6. Resistance to growth increases stress, but resilience becomes one of your most valuable assets. Every difficult season enhances your ability to handle future hardships.

7. A clear sense of purpose anchors your attitude in the middle of life's storms. If we're willing to look deeper, we'll see that life's biggest challenges bring our real hopes and desires to the surface. If they align with God's purposes, that's great. If not, we need to choose His agenda and put ours on the shelf.

8. Pay forward what you've learned so others can have constant hope on their journeys. They become your "joy and crown," your legacy, and your fondest memories.

Rubbing Off on Others

I've heard people say that each of us becomes the product of the five people we spend the most time with. Solomon put it this way: "He who walks with wise men will be wise, but the companion of fools will be destroyed" (Proverbs 13:20). A millennium later Paul wrote a corrective letter to the Christians in Corinth because envy, factions, and manipulation marked their relationships. He rebuked them for their pettiness and bad attitudes, and he painted a picture of how the body of Christ honors every person. Near the end of the letter, he reminded them that Solomon was right: "Do not be deceived: 'Evil company corrupts good character'" (1 Corinthians 15:33).

Attitude is caught more than taught. As a pastor, I want my messages to be full of grace and truth, pointing people to our hope for today and for eternity, but if I didn't live out that hope in my relationships with my family, friends, and people in the church, my message would be invalidated. After Paul left Philippi, he traveled to the coastal city of Thessalonica. He faced fierce opposition again, and he was only there for three weeks. Still, those weeks weren't spent in fear of attacks or in resentment toward God for not giving him an easier life. Even in the middle of his life being threatened, Paul poured out love on the new believers. I love the parallel passages in his first letter to the little church. First, he compares his love for them this way: "But we were gentle among you, just as a nursing mother cherishes her own children. So, affectionately longing for you, we were well pleased to impart to you not only the gospel of God, but also our own lives, because you had become dear to us." This tough, hard-nosed, goal-oriented, go-for-broke church planter was as tender as a nursing mother, offering them more than the message of the gospel—giving them his own heart "because [they] had become dear to [him]."

Immediately following this description of his tender affection for them, Paul shares that his love is also strong and clear: "You are witnesses, and God also, how devoutly and justly and blamelessly we behaved ourselves among you who believe; as you know how we exhorted, and comforted, and charged every one of you, as a father does his own children, that you would walk worthy of God who calls you into His own kingdom and glory" (1 Thessalonians 2:7–8, 10–12). His affection as a mother was tender and sweet; his affection as a father gave them clear direction.

Isn't that the kind of mentor you want? Isn't that the kind of mentor you want to be for your family and those around you?

"Give Me That Mountain!"

Soon after Moses led God's people out of slavery in Egypt, he wanted a scouting report on their destination, Canaan, the Promised Land. He selected twelve men and gave them clear instructions: "Go through the Negev and then into the mountain region. See what the land is like and whether the people living there are strong or weak, few or many. Is the land they live in good or bad? Do their cities have walls around them or not? Is the soil rich or poor? Does the land have trees or not? Do your best to bring back some fruit from the land" (Numbers 13:17–20, GW).

They were gone for forty days. When they returned, they gave their report to Moses, Aaron, and the entire community:

> We went to the land where you sent us. It really is a land flowing with milk and honey. Here's some of its fruit. But the people who live there are strong, and the cities have walls and are very large. We even saw the descendants of Anak there. The Amalekites live in the Negev. The Hittites, Jebusites, and Amorites live in the mountain region. And the Canaanites live along the coast of the Mediterranean Sea and all along the Jordan River.
> —Numbers 13:27–29, GW

Notice the optimism and realism. The land they saw was incredibly fruitful. When they said, "Here's some of its fruit," they were showing a bunch of grapes so huge that two men had to carry it between them on a pole! But yes, many tribes lived in the region—tribes that would need to be defeated, including "the descendants of Anak," who were giants.

Caleb, one of the twelve who had seen everything, was the first to voice his conviction: "Let's go now and take possession of the land. We should be more than able to conquer it" (Numbers 13:30, GW).

But ten of the spies disagreed. To make their point stronger, they spread lies saying that taking the land was impossible. Any hope they'd felt before leaving on their scouting mission was crushed under their fear and cowardice. They concluded, "We felt as small as grasshoppers, and that's how we must have looked to them" (Numbers 13:33, GW).

Moses followed the majority opinion. Instead of the journey taking about eleven days, they spent forty years wandering in the wilderness. During that time, everyone in that generation died—all but two: Joshua and Caleb, the spies who inspired faith and courage by advising them to take the land immediately.

Four decades later, Joshua became Moses' leadership heir, leading God's people across the Jordan. For five years, they fought the armies of the people inhabiting the land. Joshua allotted parcels of land to each of the tribes of Israel. After fighting to secure land for everyone else, Caleb chose that moment to claim his prize. He reminded the people that he had trusted God forty-five years earlier and advised them to take the land, but ten spies doubted. God had promised him a particular parcel in the Promised Land, and it was time to take it. He was eighty-five years old, but he had lost none of his optimism. He wasn't ready for a rocking chair. He told them, "As yet I am as strong this day as on the day that Moses sent me; just as my strength was then, so now is my strength for war, both for going out and for coming in." Then, surely with fire in his eyes and passion in his voice, Caleb announced his intentions: "Now therefore, give me this mountain of which the Lord spoke in that day; for you heard in that day how the Anakim were there, and that the cities were great and fortified. It may be that the Lord will be with me, and I shall be able to drive them out as the Lord said" (Joshua 14:11–12).

Think of the previous forty-five years for Caleb. He believed God when others doubted; he endured the struggles in the wilderness, knowing every day that it didn't have to be this way; he fought for five years to secure everyone else's land; and then he found the stamina, courage, and fierce optimism to take what had been promised to him.

Caleb is a prime case study in having a relentlessly positive attitude.

In the Crucible

When Pilate sentenced Jesus to be crucified, He was nailed to a cross between two men. We know them as "thieves," but that's probably not the whole story. A more accurate term is "brigands" or rebels. The third cross had been meant for someone else that day. Barabbas had been arrested and convicted of rebellion and murder, precisely the kind of crimes the Romans punished with crucifixion. It was the custom of the Roman governor to free one prisoner at the Jewish feast of Passover as a gesture of goodwill to the oppressed population. That fateful morning, Pilate gave them a choice: he could free either Jesus or Barabbas. They chose Barabbas. He was set free, and Jesus was nailed to the cross that had been meant for a felon. One of the ironies of this scene is that *Barabbas* means "son of the father." So, the Son of the Father took the place of the son of the father and died in his place—the guiltless for the guilty. That's a perfect picture of the doctrine of substitutionary atonement.

On Golgotha, Barabbas' two gang members hung beside the Savior. Crucifixion was a particularly gruesome form of torture. As the pain of the three men intensified and they grew weaker, something amazing happened. One of the brigands mocked Him, "If You are the Christ, save Yourself and us." But the other man noticed that Jesus' attitude toward His unjust suffering, His love for the people who had come to show their love one last time, and even His love for the executioners were different from anything he'd ever seen. He turned his head to the other brigand and gave him an accurate perspective: "Do you not even fear God, seeing you are under the same condemnation? And we indeed justly, for we receive the due reward of our deeds; but this Man has done nothing wrong." Then he said to Jesus, "Lord, remember me when You come into Your kingdom."

Jesus, undoubtedly with exquisite tenderness amid His excruciating pain, told him, "Assuredly, I say to you, today you will be with Me in Paradise" (Luke 23:39–43).

A couple of decades later, Paul told the Christians in Philippi, "Let this mind be in you which was also in Christ Jesus" (Philippians 2:5). "Mind" here is attitude: Have the same attitude as Jesus, trusting the Father in the midst of enormous suffering and finding good even in the most horrific act in history.

How can we experience a lifelong journey of having the attitude of Christ? Only by understanding His purpose. After the writer to the Hebrews lists the "heroes of the faith," he turns to the ultimate hero:

> Therefore we also, since we are surrounded by so great a cloud of witnesses, let us lay aside every weight, and the sin which so easily ensnares us, and let us run with endurance the race that is set before us, looking unto Jesus, the author and finisher of our faith, who for the joy that was set before

> Him endured the cross, despising the shame, and has sat down at the right hand of the throne of God. For consider Him who endured such hostility from sinners against Himself, lest you become weary and discouraged in your souls.
> —Hebrews 12:1–3

What was "the joy that was set before Him"? It wasn't riches. He created the universe, so all the gold, silver, oil, real estate, and jewels on every star and planet were already His. It wasn't acceptance. He was the ultimate insider in the Trinity, enjoying immeasurable affection for all eternity. His joy, His purpose, and His motivation for going to the cross were *you* and *me*. We are so valuable to Him that nothing could shake His determined attitude to demonstrate His love for us—even the torture and public shame of hanging on a criminal's cross. If He endured all that for us, then our pessimism and hopelessness can be fully washed away by His tenacious love. The Spirit can strengthen us so our attitudes remain positive no matter what challenges and heartaches we face.

From before Jesus' birth, God planned to rescue fallen humanity. During His life, He was a refugee as a child and misunderstood and mocked in His ministry. The rest of us were born to live, but Jesus was born to die—not in despair but in love for us. And eternity with Him will show us even more of His astonishing love, kindness, truth, justice, and compassion.

We can always find plenty of easy excuses for pessimism, but they leave us sour, empty, and angry. My mother showed me that it's possible to live without excuses, to search for and find the good in every circumstance. Jesus chose His attitude at every twist and turn in His life, and He has given us the wonderful privilege and responsibility of managing our attitudes in every moment.

Consider this:

1. What difference would it make if you eradicated the word *can't* from your vocabulary?

2. Review the "positivity principles." Which one(s) are you doing well? Which one(s) need(s) some attention? What steps can you take to improve them?

3. If Paul could be as gentle as a nursing mother and as encouraging as a loving father, what kind of person should you be in your most important relationships? What specific changes need to happen? What changes would the people close to you say need to happen in you?

4. Look at the passage in Joshua. Caleb had plenty of reasons to bail out on God's promise over the grueling forty years in the wilderness and five years of combat, but his attitude remained positive. What lessons can you draw from his example?

5. What does the account of Jesus and the two men crucified with Him tell us about His attitude when He suffered unjustly?

6. What are the two most important concepts you've learned from this book? How will you implement them? What difference will they make?

"MANAGING YOUR ATTITUDE IS A LIFELONG PURSUIT, NOT A SINGLE DECISION."

USING *THE SHIFT THAT CHANGES EVERYTHING* IN CLASSES AND GROUPS

This book is designed for individual study, small groups, and classes. The best way to absorb and apply these principles is for each person to study individually, answer the questions at the end of each chapter, and then discuss them in a group environment.

Order enough copies of the book for each person to have a copy.

A recommended schedule for a small group or class might be:

Week 1: Introduce the material. As a group leader, tell your story of growing in having a more positive, hopeful attitude; share your hopes for the group; and provide books for each person. Encourage people to read the assigned chapter each week and answer the questions.

Weeks 2–11: Each week, introduce the topic and share a story of how God has used the principles in your life. Lead people through a discussion of the questions at the end of the chapter.

- **Personalize each lesson.**

Don't feel pressured to cover every question in your group discussions. You may have time for all of them, but if not, pick out the three or four that had the biggest impact on you, and focus on those, or ask people in the group to share their responses to the questions that meant the most to them that week.

Make sure you personalize the principles and applications. At least once in each group meeting, share your own story to illustrate a particular point.

When you read a passage, make the Scriptures come alive. Far too often we read the Bible like a phone book, with little or no emotion. Paint a vivid picture for people. Provide insights into the risks and power of authentic relationships, and help those in your group sense the emotions of specific people in each scene.

- **Focus on application.**

The questions at the end of each chapter and your encouragement for group members to be authentic will help your group take big steps in applying the principles they're learning. Share how you are applying the principles in particular chapters each week, and encourage them to take steps of growth too.

- **Three types of questions**

If you've led groups for a few years, you already understand the importance of using open-ended questions to stimulate discussion. Three types of questions are *limiting, leading,* and *open*. Many of the questions at the end of each lesson are open-ended questions.

Limiting questions focus on an obvious answer, such as, "What does Jesus call Himself in John 10:11?" They don't stimulate reflection or discussion. If you want to use questions like these, follow them with thought-provoking, open questions.

Leading questions require the listener to guess what the leader has in mind, such as, "Why did Jesus use the metaphor of a shepherd in John 10?" (He was probably alluding to a passage in Ezekiel, but many people don't know that.) The teacher who asks a leading question has a definite answer in mind. Instead of asking this kind of question, you should simply teach the point and then ask an open-ended question about the point you have made.

Open questions usually don't have right or wrong answers. They stimulate thinking and are far less threatening because the person answering doesn't risk ridicule for being wrong. These questions often begin with "Why do you think…?" or "What are some reasons that…?" or "How would you have felt in that situation?"

- **Preparation**

As you prepare to teach this material in a group, consider these steps:

Carefully and thoughtfully read the book. Make notes; highlight key sections, quotes, or stories; and complete the reflection section at the end of each chapter. This will familiarize you with the entire scope of the content.

As you prepare for each week's group, read the corresponding chapter again and make additional notes.

Tailor the amount of content to the time allotted. You may not have time to cover all the questions, so pick the ones that are most pertinent.

Add your own stories to personalize the message and add impact.

Before and during your preparation, ask God to give you wisdom, clarity, and power. Trust Him to use your group to change people's lives.

Most people will get far more out of the group if they read the chapter and complete the reflection each week. Order books before the group or class begins or after the first week.

ACKNOWLEDGMENTS

To my amazing wife, **Tonia**—thank you. Your love, encouragement, and quiet strength carried me through every step of this book. You believed in the message, stood beside me, and reminded me why it mattered. I'm so grateful for your heart, your prayers, and your constant support. I couldn't have done this without you.

To my Lord and Savior, **Jesus Christ**—You are everything. This book, this calling, this life—it's all because of You. Your grace sustains me, Your voice guides me, and Your purpose gives meaning to everything I do. I pray this book reflects even a small portion of Your goodness and brings glory to Your name.

To the outstanding publishing team at **Harp & Sword**—thank you for helping shape this book with care, insight, and excellence. Your collaborative spirit, thoughtful suggestions, and tireless work made this process not only smooth but enjoyable. It was a privilege to work with such a gifted and dedicated team.

To the incredible people of **Center Pointe Church**—I love you more than words can express. You are my family, my joy, and my inspiration. Pastoring you is one of the greatest honors of my life. Thank you for your constant encouragement, prayers, and belief in the vision God has given us. You make ministry a joy.

And to **every reader holding this book**—thank you. I pray these pages stir something in your heart and draw you closer to the One who created you, loves you, and has a purpose for your life.

ENDNOTES

1   Brené Brown, *The Gifts of Imperfection* (Hazelden Publishing, 2010).

2   "Attitude: A Settled Way of Thinking or Feeling About Something," SafeSetters, accessed September 20, 2025, https://safesetters.com/blog/Attitude.

3   Viktor Frankl, *Man's Search for Meaning* (Beacon Press, 2006), 66.

4   Frederick Buechner, *Wishful Thinking: A Seeker's ABC* (HarperOne, 1993).

5   Timothy Keller, "The God Who Is Generous," Redeemer City to City, October 25, 2018, https://medium.com/redeemer-city-to-city/the-god-who-is-generous-7e83d26406f1.

6   Corrie ten Boom, *The Hiding Place* (Old Tappan: Spire, 1971), 238.

7   J. R. R. Tolkien, *The Lord of the Rings: The Return of the King* (Random House, 1955), 246.

8   Cornelius Plantinga Jr., "Sin: Not the Way It's Supposed to Be," Carl. F. H. Henry Center for Theological Understanding, accessed September 20, 2025, https://henrycenter.tiu.edu/wp-content/uploads/2014/01/Cornelius-Plantinga_Sin.pdf.

9   Churchill's speech before the House of Commons, June 4, 1940, International Churchill Society, accessed September 20, 2025, https://winstonchurchill.org/resources/speeches/1940-the-finest-hour/we-shall-fight-on-the-beaches/.

10   Rebecca Randall, "Wayne Grudem Changes Mind About Divorce in Cases of Abuse," *Christianity Today*, November 26, 2019, https://www.christianitytoday.com/2019/11/complementarian-wayne-grudem-ets-divorce-after-abuse/.

11   Quotes cited in "26 Brilliant Quotes on the Power of Words," *Inc.*, November 5, 2015, https://www.inc.com/peter-economy/26-brilliant-quotes-on-the-super-power-of-words.html.

12   Lewis Smedes, *Forgive and Forget* (Harper & Row, 1984), 79–80.

13   Timothy Keller, *The Reason for God* (Penguin, 2009), 196.

14   Gregory W. Lester, "Why Beliefs Are Hard to Change," *NewsLog*, October 19, 2009, https://newslog.cyber-journal.org/gregory-w-lester-why-beliefs-are-hard-to-change/.

15   "Biography of Nelson Mandela," Nelson Mandela Foundation, accessed September 20, 2025, https://www.nelsonmandela.org/biography.

16   Truth and Reconciliation Commission, accessed September 20, 2025, https://www.justice.gov.za/trc/.

17   Francis Anderson, *Job: An Introduction and Commentary* (IVP Academic, 2008), 65.

18   Zaretta L. Hammond, *Culturally Responsive Teaching and the Brain* (Corwin, 2014), part 1.

19   Lewis B. Smedes, "Forgiveness: The Power to Change The Past," *Christianity Today*, January 7, 1983, https://www.christianitytoday.com/2002/12/forgiveness-power-to-change-past-2/.

20   C. S. Lewis, *A Grief Observed* (HarperOne, 2015), 52.

21   Elisabeth Kübler-Ross, *Death: The Final Stage of Growth* (Scribner, 2009), Kindle.

22   Josh Schrock, "Tiger Woods Completes Improbable Comeback, Wins 2019 Masters Championship," NBC Sports, April 14, 2019, https://www.nbcsportsbayarea.com/news/tiger-woods-completes-improbable-comeback-wins-2019-masters-championship/1305909/#:~:text=The%20greatest%20comeback%20in%20sports%20history%20was,fifth%20Masters%20title%2C%20finishing%20at%2013%2Dunder%20par.

23   Anthony Castrovince, "How Jim Morris' Unlikely Story Became a Hit Movie," MLB.com, September 18, 2023, https://www.mlb.com/news/featured/jim-morris-story-stars-dennis-quaid-in-the-rookie#:~:text=%E2%80%9CJim%20Morris%20is%20the%20most%20improbable%20story,few%20good%20innings%20from%20making%20the%20Show.%E2%80%9D

24   Joni Eareckson Tada, "Is God Really in Control," Joni and Friends, 1987, 1.

25   N. T. Wright, *Into the Heart of Romans* (Zondervan, 2023), 154–158.

26   Augustine, *Sermons* 191.1.

27   Alexander Sarch, *Criminally Ignorant* (Oxford University Press, 2019), 13.

28   Vaish, Grossmann, and Woodward, "Not All Emotions Are Created Equal: The Negativity Bias in Social-Emotional development," *Psychological Bulletin* 134, no. 3 (2008): 383–403, https://doi.org/10.1037/0033-2909.134.3.383.

29   Helen Keller, *The Story of My Life* (Dover Publications, 1996), chapter 6.

ABOUT THE AUTHOR

Ted Pagel Jr. is the founding pastor of Center Pointe Church in Ocean Springs, Mississippi, where he has faithfully served for almost two decades. A respected Bible teacher, preacher, and leader, Pastor Ted is known for his passionate, Spirit-led messages and unwavering commitment to helping people reach their full potential in Christ.

He is deeply devoted to the love of his life, Tonia, with whom he shares a beautiful legacy of six children and nine grandchildren. His greatest joys in life are faith, family, and seeing lives transformed by the power of God.

A lover of people and a shepherd at heart, Pastor Ted has mentored countless leaders and continues to inspire generations to walk boldly in their God-given callings.

DISCOVER MORE FROM TED PAGEL

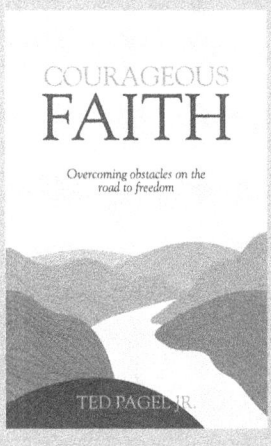

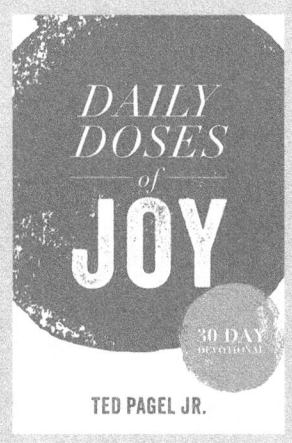

COURAGEOUS FAITH

Find the strength to face your battles, overcome fear, and walk in God's freedom.

DAILY DOSES OF JOY

Start each day grounded in gratitude, peace, and the unshakable joy of God's presence.

For these and other resources visit **TedPagelMinistries.org**.

www.ingramcontent.com/pod-product-compliance
Lightning Source LLC
LaVergne TN
LVHW020435070526
838199LV00032B/634/J